SONS OF THE ESTABLISHMENT

UNITED STATES
MEXICO
Chihuahua
Rio Grande
Houston
New Orleans
Nuevo Laredo
Laredo
Torreón
Monterrey
Durango
SIERRA MADRE ORIENTAL
San Luis Potosí
Tampico
Guadalajara
Mexico City
Puebla
Veracruz
Acapulco
Oaxaca
GULF OF MEXICO
TROPIC OF CANCER
FLORIDA
Tampa
Miami
Nassau
BAHAMA ISLANDS
ATLANTIC OCEAN
Havana
CUBA
Isle of Pines
Camagüey
Santiago de Cuba
WEST INDIES
HISPANIOLA
HAITI
DOMINICAN REPUBLIC
Port-au-Prince
Santo Domingo
San Juan
PUERTO RICO
Virgin Islands
Leeward Islands
Guadeloupe
Martinique
Windward Is.
JAMAICA
Kingston
Mérida
Yucatan Peninsula
BRITISH HONDURAS
GUATEMALA
Guatemala
HONDURAS
Tegucigalpa
San Salvador
EL SALVADOR
NICARAGUA
Managua
CENTRAL AMERICA
CARIBBEAN SEA
COSTA RICA
San José
Limón
Panama Canal
PANAMA
Panamá
Barranquilla
Cartegena
Medellín
COLOMBIA
Maracaibo
Mérida
Curaçao
Caracas
Barcelona
Port-of-Spain
TRINIDAD AND TOBAGO
Grenada
Orinoco River
Ciudad Bolívar
VENEZUELA
North Latitude
100°
90°
80°
70°
60°
20°
10°

SONS OF THE ESTABLISHMENT:

Elite Youth in Panama and Costa Rica

Daniel Goldrich

University of Oregon

Rand McNally and Company

Chicago

STUDIES IN POLITICAL CHANGE

MYRON WEINER, *Editor*

Bayley, *Public Liberties in the New States*
Goldrich, *Sons of the Establishment: Elite Youth in Panama and Costa Rica*
Zolberg, *Creating Political Order: The Party-States of West Africa*

Printed in U.S.A. by Rand McNally & Company
Library of Congress Catalog Card Number 66:19445

FOR

R. AND E., T. AND M.

PREFACE

THIS COMPARATIVE STUDY DEALS WITH THE SONS OF INCUMBENT elites in two of the world's poorer countries, Panama and Costa Rica, which are under increasing pressure for major social and political changes. These are the people who now stand to inherit the establishment, and thus the direction of future political change will probably be mightily affected by their support of, acquiescence in, or opposition to the existing political system, their conception of what needs to be changed, and how best to implement such changes. In the Panamanian case, it has been possible to assess these orientations at two points in time, so that the impact of national and international political events can be related in quasi-natural experimental fashion to changes in the political morale of the probable inheritors of the establishment. These major political events include an unprecedentedly reformist national government, the Alliance for Progress, and the consolidation of the Cuban Revolution within the Communist bloc. Assessments are made of the relationship between orientations toward the legitimacy of the political system and reformism, nationalism, internationalism of the poor nations, democratic constitutionalism, and acceptance of violence and coercion.

At a time when political sociological survey research is becoming an extremely sensitive matter in international politics, I want to express my appreciation for the high degree of cooperation I received as an independent social scientist in conducting this research. I am especially grateful to the students and staff of the schools on which the study is based for their time and consideration. Rick and Elena Beck in San José and Edward W. Scott, Jr., in Panama, because of their friendship and commitment to increased political sociological knowledge, gave me assistance in data collection without which the study could not have been done. Will Wroth assisted me in later phases of the research. Financial support was given by the University of Oregon's Institute for Community Studies, Institute of International Studies and Overseas Administration, and Center for the Advanced Study of Educational Administration, and Michigan State University's Bureau of Social and Political Research and Office of International Programs. Marshall N. Goldstein provided both grilling criticism and constant encouragement, and I am especially indebted to him.

D. G.

TABLE OF CONTENTS

LIST OF TABLES

Chapter VI

Appendix A

Appendix B

Appendix C

LIST OF FIGURES

CHAPTER I

SONS OF THE ESTABLISHMENT AND POLITICAL CHANGE

THIS IS A REPORT ON WELL-OFF HIGH SCHOOL STUDENTS, THE probable inheritors of the establishment in two Latin American countries, and their orientations on important aspects of their political systems. One of the polities is Costa Rica, generally considered one of the very few examples in Latin America of stability, adherence to constitutional democracy, and progressivism. The other is Panama, generally considered one of the area's more problematical political cases, characterized by instability, inconsistent constitutionalism, and a politics of stagnation with regard to wealth and status and power.

The report describes the political orientations of well-off secondary school students with a view to estimating their future relationship to processes of political change. The morale of the social strata represented by the students will be assessed in relation to theoretical formulations on revolution that have been developed in the field of political sociology. Though revolution is a rare phenomenon in human history, this assessment seems particularly called for because so many observers of Latin American politics have predicted, usually on most unsystematic bases, that social revolution will sweep the region. But prospects for revolution will be described as only one aspect of "the politics of legitimacy" in these countries, that is, the causes and consequences of a particular constellation of supportive, acquiescent, and oppositionalist orientations toward the political system.

The report is based on one survey in Costa Rica, in the fall of 1962, and two in Panama, the first in the summer of 1961, the second in the fall of 1963. The two measurements in the latter country, which is the more problematic polity of the two, and possibly the more useful for a comprehension of the factors underlying political change in Latin America, permit an analysis of two highly significant political experiments—the Alliance for Progress, and the Chiari administration's responses to rising demands for change (Chiari was President from October, 1960, to October, 1964). Both of these political experiments will be analyzed and evaluated in relation to the shifting patterns of political orientations of the sons of the elite.

THE UPPERDOG AND POLITICAL CHANGE

The justification for a study of the probable inheritors of the establishment is that they are the closest to political power, and they have the best chance, at this time, of exercising effective influence in future political decision-making. Obvious, and yet much of the study of political change has focused first on the currently powerless or less powerful, on their discontents and prospects for future success. In the study of revolution, for example, despite the recognition of the critical role of radical leaders of relatively privileged background, such as Castro or Lenin, there is little in the way of comparative study of incumbent elites and the conditions under which they maintained their position or were washed away in the debris of history. This is not to argue against the usefulness of the increasing number of studies of the middle and lower classes in Latin American politics, but only to affirm the logic of inclusion of *los de arriba* in the calculus of political change.

One of the most significant characteristics of the Latin American political systems is the relative stability of the power structure and of the capacity of the aristocracy and the new-rich to accommodate one another so as to maintain elitist structures committed in high degree to the interests of the wealthy and the prestigious. The factors that seem at least in large part to account for this stability include: the intense resistance to change on the part of the establishment; the tendency of many middle-class people to mold their values after those of the traditional elite;[1] the increasing fear on the part of former reformists and even radicals of the middle class that the forces of social change once unleashed will elevate Jacobins to leadership positions and

---

[1]See Frederick B. Pike, *Chile and the United States: 1880-1962* (Notre Dame: University of Notre Dame Press, 1963), throughout but particularly ch. 10; and Claudio Veliz, "Obstacles to Reform in Latin America," *The World Today*, XIX (January, 1963), 18-29.

destroy the middle class, a perspective undoubtedly heightened by the experience of the Cuban Revolution; the continued, widespread non-politicization of the lower class, even in metropolitan, industrial centers;[2] and the decision on the part of dominant military sectors to support the status quo, rather than take a risk on changes threatening both to their traditional perquisites and to their very existence (again, the specter of the Cuban experience).[3]

Under these circumstances, it is possible that a continued high level of unity on the part of the establishment in behalf of the status quo will maintain the Latin American political systems for many years to come against the relatively weak, fractionalized proponents of change. In those few countries where the political system seems to be highly legitimate, and where the establishment joins in support of the system, gradual change may be possible. If, however, the establishment loses its moral integration and a substantial segment of it begins to reject traditional positions, then massive political change may be promoted. The political psychology of the establishment is considered by Crane Brinton to be one of the critical variables in the development of revolutions. Among the several uniformities he found in his study of four great revolutions was the demoralization of groups such as those under present consideration. "... what may be called the ruling class seems in all four of our societies to be divided and inept." When "numerous and influential" people of this class begin to think their power lacks justification, or that their traditional class beliefs are wrong or irrelevant, "they are not likely to resist successfully any serious attacks on their social, economic, and political position."[4]

Brinton emphasizes that such mavericks must be numerous and conspicuous before they contribute to a state of disequilibrium. This study focuses on the political psychology of those Panamanians and Costa Ricans "scheduled" to inherit the establishment in order to assess the divisions, the demoralization, the extent of verbalized commitment to fundamental changes. If there are mavericks, their numbers and capacity for action can be assessed, but the assumption is

[2]See my "Toward the Comparative Study of Politicization, with Special Reference to Latin America," in Dwight B. Heath and Richard N. Adams (eds.), *Contemporary Cultures and Societies of Latin America* (New York: Random House, 1965), pp. 361-78.

[3]Edwin Lieuwen, *Generals vs. Presidents: Neomilitarism in Latin America* (New York: Praeger, 1965).

[4]Crane Brinton, *The Anatomy of Revolution* (New York: Vintage Books, 1957), pp. 53, 54.

made that the youths in question are or will be relatively "conspicuous," for their stratum forms a very small part of their societies; it is intensely visible and concentrated geographically in the capital city.

* * *

There are of course problems involved in the interpretation of data collected from the sons of the establishment during their secondary school years. At that point they are relatively young and inexperienced, and we do not yet know how significant the ideas held at that age and stage of life are for their future states of mind and political behavior. Recent work on political socialization, primarily in the United States and Western Europe, suggests that much of the individual's basic orientation to politics may be formed by adolescence.[5] On the other hand, major shifts in orientation can conceivably be brought about later in life by, for example, an abrupt restructuring of the environment, as in the case of the impact of social revolutions. (The role of the Castro government in the politicization of the Cuban people would be a worthwhile focus for inquiry in this regard.[6]) In the absence of longitudinal studies of political socialization in societies that have experienced or are likely to experience such abrupt and sweeping changes, estimates of the significance of adolescents' political orientations vis-à-vis their future orientations and behavior remain poorly based speculations. We do know, however, that the political orientations and behavior of secondary level students have frequently been critically important in the politics of the Latin American countries, as well as others of the same general type of economy and culture. They are actually or potentially a highly significant political group. Furthermore, there is a special aspect of the situation of the sons of the establishment—particularly the oppositionalists among them—that heightens their political significance. Their family position within the elite tends to protect them, when they articulate novel or unaccepted

[5]See, for example, Herbert Hyman, *Political Socialization* (New York: The Free Press, 1959), and David Easton and R. D. Hess, "Youth and the Political System," in Seymour M. Lipset and Leo Lowenthal (eds.), *Culture and Social Character* (New York: The Free Press, 1961), pp. 226-51.

[6]See the highly suggestive work of Richard Fagen, "International Politics and the Making of Citizens: The Case of Cuba," concerning the Cuban analysis and the comment on the study of political socialization, in the appendix to the paper (presented to the American Political Science Association, Chicago, September, 1964).

points of view, from the severe sanctions frequently meted out to dissidents. This promotes their capacity to bring about change.[7]

Given the level of resources available to me at the onset of this research, a further problem was the availability of the sons of the "upperdogs" of the two societies. Particularly in Panama but also in Costa Rica, as in Latin America generally, there is a tendency for young people of this social background to attend a university outside the country, often in the United States or Europe. Thus the group disperses after secondary school. Collection of data from the same groups of people past this point in the life cycle requires personal interviews, after all of the difficulties of locating individuals and establishing rapport with them. The problem is by no means insurmountable; it was, however, beyond the means of this project.

* * *

I have proposed the theoretical significance of the sons of the elite in the process of political change, and have indicated some problems in predicting their future behavior on the basis of their present orientations as adolescents. Now I propose a general conceptual framework within which the analysis of those orientations takes place.

LEGITIMACY AND POLITICIZATION: A CONCEPTUAL SCHEME FOR THE ANALYSIS OF POLITICAL CHANGE

If there is a revolution of rising expectations in Latin America and the preindustrial world generally, there is at the same time a continuing acquiescence in misery. From social scientists concerned with political change some set of concepts and research designs is urgently needed to increase the accuracy and depth of their predictions, or at least to serve to separate the potentially inflammable situations from those of prevailing stability.

Potential revolutionaries and less extreme partisans of change

[7]See the relevant discussion in Seymour M. Lipset, "The Political Behavior of University Students in Developing Nations," *Social and Economic Studies,* XIV (March, 1965), 35.

must be identified, as a first step. This done, the analyst must assess whether they have the two orientations required (though not in themselves sufficient) for the development of a revolutionary or reformist movement—they must perceive the relevance of government and politics to their lives, and they must evaluate the existing political system as inadequate to their needs. Frequently, people who live under constant severe deprivation fail to perceive that politics has any personal relevance to them and passively accept the status quo. Thus two dimensions of the political system are suggested as critical to this area of inquiry: legitimacy and politicization. The first concerns the range of citizen orientations from support of the system through acquiescence to opposition, and the second their range from political involvement through perception of the relevance of politics to failure to perceive any relevance at all. The assessment of significant population aggregates—in Latin America, students, professionals, and the military, for example—according to their position along these two dimensions would indicate probable sources of political stability or instability. Such a design applied to students, intellectuals, and similar people approaches a reduction to practical application of Crane Brinton's "desertion of the intellectuals" stage of revolution,[8] as well as placing these actors in the general process of political change. Where the students are from the privileged strata, they may be evaluated in regard to Brinton's "demoralization of the old elite" stage as well.

LEGITIMACY

I use the term *legitimacy* as a measure of the support a citizen accords the political system. In Easton's concept, this basic support or consensus relates to three components or "levels" of the system: the political community, the regime, and the government. *Political community* exists when "an aggregate of persons... seek to solve their problems in common through a shared political structure."[9] The *regime* is "all those arrangements that regulate the way in which the demands

[8]Brinton, *op. cit.* James C. Davies has suggested a number of ways in which conditions for revolution may be measured over time, using interviews, economic data, incidence of strikes and other events reflecting dissatisfactions; see "Toward a Theory of Revolution," *American Sociological Review,* XXVII (February, 1962), 7.

[9]Easton's development of the concepts of political community, regime, government, consensus, and legitimacy may be found in two places, "An Approach to the Analysis of Political Systems," *World Politics,* IX (April, 1957), 383-400, and "Problems in the Study of Political Socialization," a paper presented to the American Political Science Association, St. Louis, 1958. This definition of community is from the latter, p. 7. A revised version of the paper has appeared in Easton and Hess, "Youth and the Political System," *op. cit.*

put into the system are settled and the way in which decisions are put into effect. They are the so-called rules of the game. . . ."[10] The *government* is "all those roles through which the day to day formulation and administration of binding decisions for a society are undertaken."[11]

In sum, I will use *legitimacy* to indicate the extent of the citizens' belief in the appropriateness of their political system; it is conceived as a function of the extent of appropriateness attributed to the three components of the system—the political community, the regime, and the government (the decision-makers). It is, of course, a psychological variable, resulting directly from the perceptions of the citizens, not from the objective situation. Thus, it increases according to the conviction of the citizens that the decision-makers (as they perceive them) and the rules of the game (as they perceive them) are appropriate. Legitimacy will not necessarily be affected even if the citizens, through ignorance or manipulation, are wrong about who really makes the decisions, for example.

Actually, the extent to which citizens have differentiated orientations toward the three levels of the political system probably varies a great deal from one polity to another. The incidence of complex legitimacy orientations will probably vary according to the complexity of the society, the duration of the political system and, perhaps, with the concentration of power. For example, in the new nations where the rules of the game have often not become highly institutionalized, legitimacy may be largely a function of the behavior of the decision-makers. A case in point is Viet Nam where, for many citizens, the appropriateness of the system seemed closely related to their evaluation of the behavior of Ngo Dinh Diem and his immediate advisers. In that polity, the rules of the game are what the small number of top powerholders say they are. However, the great majority of the Vietnamese have practically no experience with the political process on a national level, which probably discourages the development of differentiated legitimacy orientations, regardless of the operational code of the decision-makers. The same situation obtains in many other new nations, as can be seen by the crucial importance of a leader in the maintenance or disintegration of support for the political system. A charismatic leader may, indeed, be a prerequisite for the development of legitimacy in a new nation.[12]

---

[10]"An Approach to the Analysis of Political Systems," p. 392.

[11]"Problems in the Study of Political Socialization," p. 5.

[12]Gideon Sjoberg, "Political Structure, Ideology, and Economic Development," a paper read before the Carnegie Faculty Seminar on Political and Administrative Development (Department of Government, Indiana University, 1963).

If, as I assume, the incidence of complex legitimacy orientations is variable, it is obviously desirable to develop for the research design some basic measure of legitimacy, some indicator of the citizen's general disposition to support or accept or oppose his political structure. This would be a useful instrument in the study of any political system, providing a base from which to assess and compare differentiated orientations toward political community, regime, and government.

THE MEANING OF ACQUIESCENCE

In the foregoing I have suggested the danger inherent in a concept of legitimacy formulated as a dichotomy—legitimacy or illegitimacy, with no place in between for the orientations of the many people of many states who offer neither support nor opposition to their political system. These people can be said to *acquiesce* in the system. Logically, acquiescence includes two types of citizen—the *neutral,* who feels little impulse toward support or opposition, and the *ambivalent,* who supports some aspects of the political system and opposes others. Of the politically acquiescent, the neutrals are probably the most numerous; to the chagrin of the alienated intellectual, this group very likely includes most of the world's peasants, especially in the less developed countries. If thoroughly alienated intellectuals are rare in the world, as I think is the case, a very large proportion of them seem to fall into the ambivalent category. The problems facing the new states are so overwhelming and pervasive that it is probably the rare intellectual who accords unqualified support to his political system.[13] Considering the power and influence of the intellectual in a new state, the maintenance or disintegration of the political system may rest, in large measure, on whether his orientation toward legitimacy is ambivalent or hostile.

TYPES OF LEGITIMACY DISTRIBUTION

The term legitimacy is found frequently in definitions of the political system, but usually without explication. Which of its citizens and how many of them must accept a political system as legitimate before its stability is assured? These are questions political theorists

---

[13]Edward Shils has analyzed the orientations of intellectuals toward authority in an article that is particularly apposite to the development of a theory of legitimacy: "Intellectuals in the Political Development of the New States," *World Politics,* XII (April, 1960), 329-68.

commonly bypass. Easton suggests that a very limited group of citizens is sufficient to maintain a system in equilibrium, so long as the group's membership holds a concentration of power and actively supports the system while most of the remaining citizens are neutral.[14] Such, he suggests, may be the case in India.[15] One should not, therefore, assume that in the absence of revolt a stable system is a function of widespread legitimacy. A system lacking legitimacy on the part of the mass of citizens may be stable because the latter have failed to develop an image of alternatives in contrast to which their situation might be seen as illegitimate. Such people neither accord support nor opposition to the system; rather they acquiesce, and their acquiescence seems closely related to their low level of politicization.[16] If most citizens hold their political system to be illegitimate, it is probable that power must be tightly concentrated and coercion widely used or threatened if the system is to stand.

A cursory examination of the world's political systems suggests that few are accorded legitimacy by the majority of their citizens. It is probable that some or all of the following factors would be prerequisite to such a general accordance of legitimacy: strong political traditions (as in the United States, Great Britain, and the Soviet Union), euphoria resulting from a revolution or potent nationalist movement (as in the early stages of the Cuban Revolution[17] or the period of the

---

[14]A parallel problem in (Parsonian) social systems analysis has been treated by Frank C. Nall, II. He suggests that a high level of moral integration may not be so critical an aspect of the maintenance of order in large-scale social systems as Parsons' writings would suggest. "It may well be that key roles, collectivities, or classes have a far greater significance for the maintenance of stability and order in a highly differentiated and segregated society than does universal or widespread consensus of moral values." See his "Role Expectations: A Cross-cultural Study," *Rural Sociology,* XXVII (March, 1962), 41.

[15]"An Approach to the Analysis of Political Systems."

[16]A comment relevant to this area of political theory has been made by Melvin Tumin concerning assumptions in social systems analysis about general social consensus. Advising against making assumptions about consensus simply because no action has been taken to change a situation, he writes: "In the more general case, it is probably true that subordinate peoples' failure to act to improve their situation is as much due to their inability to conceive of a possible alternative and/or, when they do conceive and desire alternatives, to contrive ways to carry out these ideas." *Social Class and Social Change in Puerto Rico* (Princeton: Princeton University Press, 1961), p. 480.

[17]Richard Fagen has analyzed the role of Castro's appeal to Cuban nationalism in the creation of a high degree of legitimacy of the revolutionary political system in "Calculation and Emotion in Foreign Policy: the Cuban Case," *Conflict Resolution,* VI (September, 1962), 214-21. Evidence as of 1960 in support of Fagen's thesis is presented in Lloyd A. Free, "Attitudes of the Cuban People toward the Castro Regime" (Princeton: The Institute for International Social Research, 1960) (mimeographed).

late thirties and early forties in Germany), or increasingly effective action by government to meet the citizens' perceived needs (as in the United States or the Soviet Union).[18] Systems presumably possessing a high degree of accorded legitimacy today are the Scandinavian nations, the United States, Great Britain, Canada, Uruguay, the Philippines, Malaya, and the Soviet Union. The basic point to notice, however, is the relative rarity of such systems. The most frequent pattern of legitimacy orientations is probably the one wherein the bulk of the citizenry simply acquiesces.

In Latin America there seem to be few systems whose citizens accord them either widespread legitimacy or illegitimacy. Even a traditional political democracy like Chile, which has exhibited a high degree of consensus in the past, now shows rising dissatisfaction with the regime and the decision-makers.[19] The only countries in the region which I could, even in speculation, place in the category of systems broadly accorded legitimacy are Uruguay and Costa Rica, and the Uruguayan system has become more problematic with the acceleration of economic decline. On the other hand, there are few clearly consignable to the broadly illegitimate category, Paraguay being the most clear cut, with Haiti next. Even the Dominican Republic under Trujillo is hard to categorize because, despite the fervent opposition of part of the urban middle class, there was also apparently rather widespread acquiescence toward the Benefactor. Nationalism has been mentioned as a factor tending to promote legitimacy, but nationalism in most Latin American countries has been defensive, and has thus not encouraged the development of high morale or real national pride. In the few exceptions like Mexico and Brazil, the effects of nationalism have probably been neutralized in some degree by other, countervailing factors which have reduced legitimacy—corruption, resentment of increasingly conservative social and economic policies, etc. The difficulty of speculation is a strong indication in itself of the need for comparative empirical investigation.

To analyze the relationship between legitimacy and political change most efficiently, it is desirable to focus either on the people who hold power or on those with resources that indicate a likely potential for power. For this reason, I have begun my investigation of

[18]See Seymour M. Lipset's analysis of the relationship between legitimacy and effectiveness in his *Political Man* (Garden City, New York: Doubleday, 1960), pp. 77-83.

[19]Pike, *op. cit.*

political change in Latin America by concentrating on students and intellectuals, a category whose political orientations and behavior have been crucial factors in the development, maintenance, and disintegration of political consensus.

POLITICIZATION

Although definitions of politics vary, there is widespread agreement that much of politics is decision-making processes. It is conventional to conceive such processes as a series of analytically distinct stages, such as, for example, policy formulation, policy deliberation, organization of political support, authoritative consideration, the decisional outcome – an event, promulgation of the outcome, and policy effectuation.[20] Some minority of the population in industrially advanced societies and a large proportion in the preindustrial and transitional societies, however, are not even in the political arena perceptually. To assess the full range of roles of citizens in their polity it is necessary to extend the conception of the decision-making process further to include a stage of political perception logically preceding policy formulation or any of the others.

One of the most significant aspects of the transition from preindustrialism is the emergence of the populace from prepoliticization to a realization that government is not immutable but can be made to meet needs. Perception of the personal relevance of government is here considered the first stage in the political process. Politicization is conceived as a continuum of individual political awareness and personal involvement in the world of politics and government.[21] This concept of politicization has two dimensions: one, the perception of the personal relevance of government, is perceptual, the other, political activity, is overt and behavioral. If the two variables are treated as analytically distinct, so that for every position on the perception of relevance scale (past the point of minimal politicization), there were two types – the politically alert spectator and the politically alert activist, for example – a more refined politicization matrix could be developed. (With regard to the present study, however, this would require a larger

[20]This conception of the process is taken from R. E. Agger, D. Goldrich, and B. E. Swanson, *The Rulers and the Ruled: Political Power and Impotence in American Communities* (New York: John Wiley, 1964), ch. 2, "A Political Decision-Making Model and Key Concepts," pp. 37-68.

[21]The quality of that political awareness, the modes of politicization, is treated in my "Toward the Comparative Study of Politicization . . .," *op. cit.*

sample than I have available, for the following reasons. The sample is sharply skewed toward high politicization, in both perception and activity, so that most of the cells in the matrix would be empty. Second, my primary concern with regard to this highly politicized sample is legitimacy orientations. Distribution of the small sample into categories of legitimacy orientations precludes the further holding constant of other variables.)

TYPES OF DISTRIBUTIONS OF POLITICIZATION

It has already been suggested that minimal politicization is more widespread in the industrial than the preindustrial or transitional societies. Sjoberg[22] describes the functioning of the preindustrial value system in the maintenance of nonpoliticization among the non-elite: the world is given, direction is provided by tradition and absolutes; thus there is relatively little impetus to look to any social institution to modify the environment. The lower class in particular lacks the variety of experience to develop a complex frame of reference, for example, a perspective on time that contrasts a future with present and past. Those of the lower class who develop such complex perspectives and therefore the capacity to feel grievances about the system are extremely vulnerable to the concentrated sanctions available to the elite. For example, the level of skills is low (technology being relatively simple), and the consequent substitutability of labor is high. The retribution exacted from the deviant politicized tends to discourage others from expectations that political activity could be fruitful.

A further factor retarding minimal politicization in the preindustrial and transitional societies is the low standard of living of the great bulk of the population. The evidence is that such conditions severely limit the capacity to engage in social interaction aside from that absolutely necessary to one's occupational and family life. Since politicization is a function of socialization, the resulting distribution of the perception of the personal relevance of government and politics would seem to be extremely limited.[23]

With industrial development comes a perception of the manipulability of the environment, including the social aspects. Industrialism

[22]*The Preindustrial City* (New York: The Free Press, 1958).

[23]For a highly relevant review of studies of the effect of levels of living on personality, including the effect of changes such as extreme deprivation, see James C. Davies, *Human Nature in Politics* (New York: John Wiley, 1963).

creates a demand for an educated labor force, and with education, a more complex perspective creating a capacity for grievances and demands. Furthermore, the more active the government in meeting situations characterized as needs, the more expectations are generated that government can meet a variety of needs.

Sanctions continue to play an important role in the transitional society[24] in that countervailing power of non-elites is extremely limited. Throughout history systematic repression has "tranquilized" many societies that were incipiently unstable because of rising expectations and frustrations.

In any event, a recent systematic study of the political culture of five countries (United States, England, Germany, Italy, and Mexico) varying by level of economic development shows the expected pattern of variation in what may be termed politicization.[25] The same pattern holds in a study of six countries within a culture area, the Middle East.[26]

Obviously the hypothesis that politicization varies with the level of economic development does not preclude further hypotheses concerning fluctuations by stages of industrial development. For example, as automation destroys the jobs of millions of skilled blue-collar workers much faster than the capacity of the society either to retrain them to meet new demands for labor or to revamp the education of the young, the technologically unemployed or unemployable and others among the culturally deprived (the youth of Harlem or Appalachia, for example) may become less oriented to the world (and political society) as manipulable and more anomic or oriented toward fate.

THE LEGITIMACY-POLITICIZATION MATRIX

A nine-cell matrix is produced by the cross-classification of legitimacy orientations and politicization (Figure I-1). The legitimacy types include supporters, acquiescers, and opponents. Politicization types may be extremely complex, but are limited here to only non-

[24]This is not to suggest that sanctions do not significantly affect the politics of industrial societies. The theoretical formulations of *The Rulers and the Ruled, op. cit.*, treat this factor as basic to the study of politics.

[25]G. Almond and S. Verba, *The Civic Culture: Political Attitudes and Democracy in Five Nations* (Princeton: Princeton University Press, 1963).

[26]Daniel Lerner, *The Passing of Traditional Society: Modernizing the Middle East* (Glencoe, Ill.: The Free Press, 1958).

Figure I-1. LEGITIMACY-POLITICIZATION MATRIX

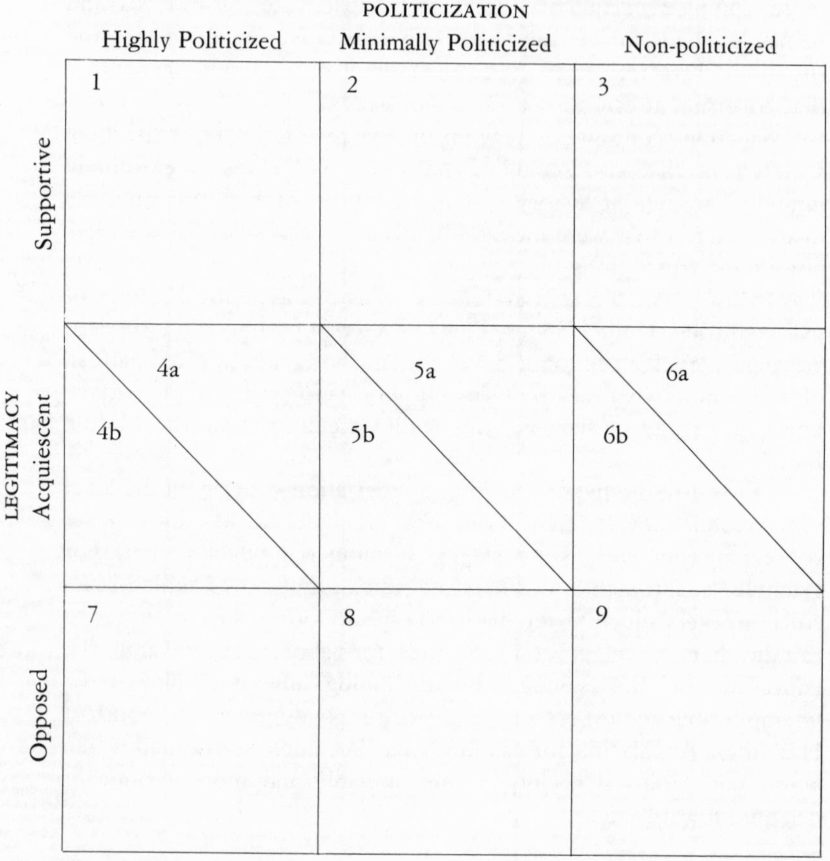

LEGITIMACY	POLITICIZATION: Highly Politicized	Minimally Politicized	Non-politicized
Supportive	1	2	3
Acquiescent	4a / 4b	5a / 5b	6a / 6b
Opposed	7	8	9

politicized (non-perceivers of the personal relevance of government and politics), minimally politicized (those who perceive governmental relevance, but are not actively involved), and the highly politicized (perceivers who are actively involved). Given the necessary data, one could locate on such a matrix entire national populations or their subgroups (such as professionals, students, and other intellectuals), or subgroups within one political system.

Where the significant groups cluster in cell 1 (Highly Politicized, Supportive), the system will tend toward stability. Where they cluster in cell 7 (Highly Politicized, Opposed), it will tend toward instability; revolutionary leaders should appear here. If citizens with power resources cluster in cell 4 (Highly Politicized, Acquiescent), it is important to determine whether their acquiescence is a function of neutrality or ambivalence. If they are ambivalent, the analyst must further ascertain the various aspects of the system they support and oppose in order to understand what changes in the system would lead to greater stability or instability. If the acquiescent in cell 4 are essentially neutral, they may constitute a kind of inertia factor. Conceivably, they will go along with any system that exists. Thus, if a counter-elite attains the power to establish a new system, these neutrals may continue to occupy a position of acquiescence. Cell 6 (Nonpoliticized, Acquiescent) would probably be the location of the mass of peasants referred to earlier.

Some cells in the matrix seem to be primarily theoretical – there are few actual situations like those such concatenations of types seem to describe. For example, it appears unlikely that there are many citizens who, seeing no personal relevance in government, feel strongly that the political system is either legitimate (cell 3) or illegitimate (cell 9). It is more believable that those who perceive no relevance in government should merely acquiesce in the political system (cell 6). There may be one possible significant exception – the tradition-bound person in the less-developed society, who might very well believe his rulers hold their position by divine right or by virtue of qualifications he has no capacity to evaluate or right to judge. To him authority is simply accepted; questioning it is, in his culture, quite inconceivable. Thus he can easily find the system legitimate, yet not feel that the world of politics and government has any personal relevance (cell 3). Such a person was probably the Turkish peasant who, asked what he would do if he were president, answered, "My God! How can you ask such a thing? How can I . . . I cannot . . . president of Turkey . . . master of the whole world?"[27] The utter irrelevance of government to this kind of person prevents him from playing a leading part in the process of political change, though he may provide an element of inertia that retards or conditions the process.

* * *

This conceptual framework provides the basis for most of the ensuing inquiry into the political orientations of the students. Before the analysis of their orientations, however, their national political systems and the methodology of the study will be described.

---

[27] *Ibid.*, p. 3.

CHAPTER II

WHO THEY ARE AND HOW THEY WERE STUDIED

THE STUDENTS ABOUT WHOM THIS STUDY REPORTS ATTEND schools operated for boys by Catholic orders. The tuition limits recruitment to the better-off sectors, although a few scholarships are provided poorer boys. The families represented at the schools are upper and upper-middle class. While it is true that many middle-class people in Latin America seek to send their children to private schools as a symbol of status and as a channel to high-level opportunities, there are other private schools available in both capital cities that charge less and that have a less prestigious clientele.

The physical character of the schools reflects their class character. Compared with other public and private secondary institutions, they have luxurious facilities, new modernistic buildings and an imposing setting in recently developed residential areas. In the case of Panama, the student bodies of the various high schools show a strong association between social class level and the color of the students. This is much less evident in the Costa Rican case because there are fewer Negroes in the area of the capital, not because a different relationship exists between class and race.

These are elite schools socially in two senses. First, each of the schools is one of a very few in each country that recruit the sons of the politically most influential, wealthy, commercial, agricultural, and professional class. The reason for selecting these particular schools from among the few in this category is simply that the two are, according to our best informants, examples of the socially most prestigious schools, and while no studies of the set of such schools are available, neither appears to represent any relevant deviance with respect to this top elite institutional status. The two sets of students, then, may be considered a purposive sample of the sons of the socioeconomic elite in Panama and Costa Rica. The second sense of eliteness derives from the fact that, of the population over 15 years of age, only 6.6 per cent of Panamanians and only 4 per cent of Costa Ricans have 10 or more years of education.[1] Thus, these and any other advanced secondary school students are members of a very small, highly advantaged educational elite.

According to the school administration, the great bulk of the students will go on to university, most of these into the professions of law, medicine, architecture, and engineering, which of course does not preclude later combination with business enterprise. This projection is matched by the students' own expectations; practically all (94 per cent of the Panamanians and 86 per cent of the Costa Ricans) say that they will attend university after completing their secondary studies, and most say that they intend to enter these professions. It is in these social positions that most of the two countries' politically most influential citizens are found.

The students' self-reports on their families provide additional evidence of their families' position in the social and political structure. They report that only a very small proportion of the fathers hold occupations classifiable as manual or working class (Costa Ricans, 9 per cent; Panamanians, 4 per cent). About one-third of the fathers are professional men (Costa Ricans, 31 per cent; Panamanians, 36 per cent), and the remainder are mainly businessmen and managers.

While less than 1 per cent of the national populations has a higher education, over half the Panamanian students' fathers and over two-fifths of the the Costa Ricans' (53 and 42 per cent, respectively) have at least attended university. Only 14 per cent of the Panamanians' fathers are reported to have only a primary school education or less, and only 18 per cent of the Costa Ricans'.

Limited information on familial possessions reflects the same privileged position as the figures above; 84 per cent of the Panamanian students' families are reported to own automobiles, as are 69 per cent of the Costa Ricans'.

The students were asked whether or not any family member or relative held a position in government or politics, and, if so, what that position was. Though some who answered affirmatively to the first neglected or chose not to respond to the second more detailed part of the query, the data that were collected reflect the established high

[1]United Nations, *Demographic Yearbook 1956*.

position of the families in their respective national political systems. Two-thirds of the Panamanians and half the Costa Ricans described some political post held by relatives, many listing several (though only one such position, the highest mentioned, was considered here). Within this group, two-thirds in both countries mentioned highest-level positions, such as president, cabinet minister, supreme court justice, or deputy in the national assembly. A substantial difference was reported between the two samples in the proportion naming relatives in the presidency or national assembly: 29 per cent of the Panamanians compared with 12 per cent of the Costa Ricans. This may reflect the more oligarchical structure of the Panamanian polity.

Data are not available concerning the extent to which the national political elites are derived from graduates of these schools. It is not expected that these two schools, particularly in the Costa Rican case, would be the only ones represented in this regard, though they would be significant. But both Panama and Costa Rica are countries in which, regardless of their differences in degree of democracy, the political decision-makers and their reference groups are recruited very heavily from the upper and upper-middle social strata, and these strata send their sons to the specific schools included in this study or others like them. This is the basis for the samples and for the characterization of the students as the probable inheritors of the establishment.

This study does not include a further inquiry into the school and family as agents of political socialization. Primarily, this is because the focus is on the psychological relationship of the probable inheritors of the establishment to the national political system, and not on the role of such agents as school and family in the production of this set of orientations. The focus is the capacity of the sons of the elite to accommodate political change, and not primarily on the factors that produce that particular capacity, with the exception of the impact of the political system variable itself.

The sample was designed, however, in such a way that assumptions could be made about the family as the key element in the future recruitment of many of the students into elite political roles. The school was not considered to be nearly so important an agency. First of all, the social-civic studies part of the curriculum is traditional; though there is politically relevant content, the schools' failure to confront the major contemporary political issues means that most students are apparently little affected by the school insofar as their political orientations are concerned. One datum provides evidence in support of this characterization of the schools, particularly vis-à-vis the family, as agents of political socialization. When asked to indicate from a list of possibilities to whom they could best go for political advice, 70 per cent or more of each group of students mentioned a family member, less than 10 per cent mentioned a teacher, and even fewer a school organization. Furthermore, given the relatively apolitical environment of these schools, in contrast to the public secondary schools which, especially in Panama, are centers of politicization and agitation, the study focuses on these students not in their role as students, but in their role as sons of the incumbent elites. While there may be considerable difference in the style of education as between the Catholic, more culturally traditional, private schools and the most modern of the public secondary schools, the two schools on which this study is based do not differ in apparent ways that might account for the particular patterns of political orientation of the two student bodies. In any event, these are secondary considerations, because the schools were used as a convenient sampling site, not because of their theoretical importance as political socialization agents.

HOW THE STUDY WAS DONE

The Costa Rican data were collected in the fall of 1962, approximately eight months after the Presidential election of that year. The first collection of data in Panama occurred in the summer of 1961, approximately fourteen months after the Presidential election of 1960. The second collection of data from this school occurred in the fall of 1963, two years and three months after the first collection, and seven months before the Presidential election of 1964. All of these data were collected after the establishment of the Cuban Revolution, the Bay of Pigs invasion, and Castro's movement into the Communist bloc. Immediately after the first data collection came the announcement of the Alliance for Progress by President Kennedy, and by the time of the second data collection, some implementation of programs under its auspices had occurred.

In all three cases, preliminary arrangements involved first contacting the rectors of the schools, explaining the nature of the study, and requesting about one hour of time during a school day for the administration of the questionnaire. It was explained that the research was the endeavor of an individual professor from a state university in the United States, that it had grown out of a program of cross-cultural political socialization research, and that the particular study was financed by one of the university's research institutes. Cooperation was readily given.

Only students in the last two years of the five-year secondary sequence were selected as respondents. The age range of the great bulk was 16 through 18, old enough to be presumed to be involved in the student political environment of their countries, as well as to have the capacity to reflect on the complex political and personal questions put to them. In all cases, this followed the advice of the school administrators and teachers.

The questionnaires were completed in each school during one day. Care was taken to assure that students in different classes and rooms could not discuss the questionnaire among themselves. There were no problems of disorder or overt confusion. In both the Costa Rican and the first Panamanian cases, completed questionnaires were obtained from over 90 per cent of the students in the selected grades. Those missed were absent, and in a very few cases, returned questionnaires were rendered useless by students obviously not willing to cooperate. Thus, for these administrations, there is little question about the representativeness of the respondents. The second Panamanian case of data collection is somewhat more problematic, in that only about 75 per cent of the students in the selected grades were given the questionnaire. In this case, however, care was taken to assure that those omitted by reason of absence and scheduling problems were not different from those responding in social background, academic performance, etc.

In all three cases, the administration of the questionnaire was directed by a student from the national university who had been serving as an assistant on the study. This person stood before the assembled student respondents, explained the auspices, purpose, and procedures of the study, answered preliminary questions, assured the students that neither their teachers nor administrators nor anyone else with the exception of the research team would see the completed questionnaires. Confidence was no doubt the more readily won by the fact that respondents were not asked to sign their names or otherwise to give identifying information. The university student assistant remained with the students during their completion of the questionnaire, but actually had no problems to resolve. The cover page of the questionnaire also described the auspices, purposes, etc. Briefly, the sponsors were described as a group of North American professors making a study in a number of countries throughout the world of students' opinions on the civic life of the nation. The statement stressed the scientific nature of the inquiry, the importance of student opinion in their countries, the dependence of the study on their free cooperation, and the maintenance of their responses in confidence. Finally, the statement indicated the manner in which the questionnaire should be filled out, etc.; this section was exceedingly short inasmuch as the questionnaire format was straightforward and apparently easily comprehended by students of this level.

THE DESIGN AND ASSUMPTIONS ABOUT CHANGE

Two measurements of opinion were made in Panama, but the design was not of the panel type. That is, data were not collected on the same individuals at two points in time. Thus this report cannot make statements about the effect of political events on particular individuals' ideas and acts. What can be presented is a comparison of the responses of two sets of people at significantly different points in time. The two sets of people are similar: they attend the same school, have the same social background, have had the same sorts of educational and general life experiences. The only theoretically significant difference, to my knowledge, is their exposure to the national government, elected in 1960. The first set of respondents were studied during the "honeymoon" of the Chiari administration. The second set provided data near the end of that administration, and in the midst of a gathering campaign for the next Presidential and legislative elections. What is of concern in this study is not individual changes in orientation, but changes within a significant sector of the population, and the association of these changes with significant political events.

The assumption is that much of the change is a function of the reaction of these students to the Chiari government over time. This cannot be conclusively tested because measurements are lacking on similar students at similar points in past time vis-à-vis other national administrations. It is possible, therefore, that changes of the sort found between 1961 and 1963 had also occurred in the past, and that what I attribute to a particular administration (and a particular foreign policy of the United States government) as an effect is spurious; the effect may only be that of a "natural tendency" of most national administrations to make enemies and fail to live up to all its promises over time. Underlying my assumption is the estimate that the Chiari government has provided a significantly different political experience for politically aware Panamanian citizens. The bases of that estimate are given in the following chapter's analysis of recent national politics. Briefly summarized, they involve the democratic nature of the 1960 election and subsequent assumption of office by the opposition, the new government's attempt to project an image of systematic and basic reforms, its public stance as an oligarchic mediator of a crisis of unfulfilled aspirations of the great mass of citizens, the reinforcement of this definition of the situation by ever-heightening "social" nationalism and by the successful, radical Cuban Revolution and its local adherents and sympathizers and the U. S. government with its Alliance for Progress.

RESPONSE SET

There have been relatively few survey-based studies of a political sociological nature on Latin America, and in those few, little apparent attempt has been made to assess the extent of response set, the systematic response by the subject to the format in which items are presented rather than to the intended substance of the items. Inasmuch as the "sociological" kind of questionnaire provided a new experience for most of the respondents (and the surveying of Latin American students' opinion a relatively new experience for the researcher), it seems incumbent on us to evaluate it from the standpoint of how well the questionnaire tapped responses to the matter raised by the items themselves, rather than simply assuming that the high degree of formal cooperation given by the students was an acceptable predictor of the validity of the responses.

The types of response set of concern here are the tendencies of some people to assent to propositions made to them and of others to reject them, in both cases regardless of the content of the propositions. A general scale of response type was developed to assess the extent of content sensitivity and the various kinds of set.[2] The general scale was itself based on two subscales which had the same format but different substance, on the assumption that some people react "sensitively" to particularly salient matters and in a "set" fashion to matters about which they lack concern. Others, of course, may react in a generally set or sensitive fashion to questionnaire stimuli.

[2]The entire procedure used in dealing with response set is described in Appendix C.

The major response set problem actually was assent, rather than either non-answering or rejection. In view of the need to control or eliminate response set to reduce the chance of making spurious statements and at the same time to maintain a sample size sufficient for the projected analysis, the decision was made to consider as Content Sensitive only those who demonstrated content sensitivity on one subscale and something less than a high degree of response set on the other. The Content Sensitive by this measure included 60 per cent of the Costa Rican sample, 60 per cent of the 1961 Panamanian sample, and 79 per cent of the 1963 Panamanian sample. Because the limited, post hoc investigation of response set indicated that the data collected from the non-content sensitive were unreliable from the standpoint of the study's theoretical focus, the decision was made to eliminate them from the subsequent analysis.[3] Even though the resulting samples are much smaller, the Content Sensitive provide a much more trustworthy basis of analysis.

[3]In the foregoing description of the occupational and political characteristics of the students' families, the data were based on responses from all the students. The items in question were open-ended, which minimized the problem of response set. Hereafter, however, the analysis is based only on the responses of the Content Sensitive.

CHAPTER III

NATIONAL POLITICAL SYSTEMS AND LEVELS OF ECONOMIC DEVELOPMENT

THE POLITICAL ORIENTATIONS OF THESE COSTA RICAN AND PANAMANIAN students can be more usefully examined after a brief consideration of the two national political systems and their respective levels of economic development.

The political history of Costa Rica reflects a high level of political stability, democratic constitutionalism, and social integration relative to Central America and to Latin America as a whole. Despite this auspicious past, Costa Rica has within recent years experienced a violent revolution (1948) reflecting an intense three-way competition among political leadership groups, which was based at least in part on intense ideological difference; the emergence of the perception of large-scale social problems and rising expectations of an expanding scope of government in the area of welfare and social policies; and the continual threat of economic decline caused by diminishing returns from agricultural exports. Thus, national politics has become far more problem-ridden than is perhaps generally realized, and the legitimacy of the political system may be given a prolonged, severe test.

Panamanian political history reflects a high level of instability of the type which Kling has characterized as Latin American political instability generally: "(1) it is chronic; (2) it frequently is accompanied by limited violence; (3) it produces no basic shifts in economic, social, or political policies."[1] In addition to the ethnic cleavage between West Indian Negroes and other citizens, there has been a low level of national integration in a geographic sense. The ethnic difference looms larger in Panama because the West Indian Negroes are concentrated

[1]Merle Kling, "Toward a Theory of Power and Political Instability in Latin America," *Western Political Quarterly*, IX (March, 1956), 21-35.

to a high degree in the major cities of Panama and Colón (and the history of racism in the adjacent Canal Zone, where many of these Negroes have worked, exacerbates political tensions), while Costa Rica's counterparts are concentrated along the Atlantic Coast away from the national population center of the *meseta central.* Despite an expanding economy in very recent years, and a standard of living that ranks high within the Latin American area, maldistribution of income, a low level of development of welfare and social policies, and the constant threat of major nationalistic uprisings vis-à-vis the Canal create severe political tensions, and the country lacks the history of political accommodations that may ease Costa Rica's future times of trial.

THE ECONOMIC DEVELOPMENT COMPLEX

The two national economies differ in that Costa Rica relies heavily on coffee and banana exports, whereas Panamanian national income depends principally on activities associated with the Canal. Otherwise, however, the economies are substantially similar in agricultural production, with the United Fruit Company as the largest firm in both countries. Heavy unemployment has been a severe problem recently in both countries, though the severity has appeared worse in Panama, particularly in the depressed Atlantic terminus of the Canal, the city of Colón. The extremely violent riots of January, 1964, along the Canal Zone border sharply exacerbated unemployment and loss of income, as businesses were wrecked, U. S. citizens resident in Panama evacuated, capital flight began, and tourism and Zonian purchases in Panama both dropped.[2]

Both Panama and Costa Rica rank high among the Latin American states on such indicators of the social structure as distribution of education. For example, they rank very close together and within the top five countries in regard to proportions of children in primary, secondary, and university educational institutions. They rank fourth and sixth in literacy – about four-fifths of the Costa Rican, and seven-tenths of the Panamanian population, are estimated as literate.[3] The

[2]For estimates of these costs to the Panamanian economy, see the *Hispanic American Report,* XVII (April, May, 1964).

[3]R. Vekemans and J. L. Segundo, "Essay of a Socio-Economic Typology of the Latin American Countries," in E. de Vries and J. Medina Echavarría (eds.), *Social Aspects of Economic Development in Latin America* (Paris: UNESCO, 1963).

difference, however, is probably more significant than it at first appears, for it is a function of differences in the extent of rural-urban integration. Urban literacy has been estimated at 92 per cent for both countries, with the rural rate lagging behind, at 72 per cent for Costa Rica and 54 per cent for Panama.[4] This suggests a greater degree of national integration for the former.

Recent estimates of the proportion of central government expenditures on education are 25.3 per cent for Costa Rica in 1963, and 28.3 per cent for Panama in 1962.[5] On the other hand, these gross statistics on the scope of government in the area of education do not show how effectively the educational system is integrated with the economy of the two countries. In this regard there is an indication of substantial differences. For example, both national economies depend heavily on agriculture, but in at least one respect the Panamanian system of higher education appears to suffer more than the Costa Rican from the cultural traditions of the preindustrial society. In 1957 the ratio of population per agricultural college graduate was 1,763 to 1 in Costa Rica, which held first rank in Latin America, and 38,933 to 1 in Panama, which ranked fourteenth.[6]

Their rankings on other indices of economic development such as the proportion of population to physicians and dentists are close to one another, but much lower in rank among the countries of the region than was the case with education. However, Costa Rica led all countries in 1952-1953 estimates of ratio of persons to hospital beds, and Panama ranked fifth.[7]

Panama ranked third in the region in per capita national income (1960 estimate), while Costa Rica ranked seventh (1961 estimate).[8] This does not reflect the character of the distribution of national income, though, and a demographic analyst has commented that "although Panamanian per capita income is high, the 1950 census showed that 60 per cent of urban workers received less than 75 balboas per month. With the balboa equal to the dollar and the economy geared to the dollar, and high taxes on basic goods, these are

---

[4] *The Educational Situation in Latin America* (Paris: UNESCO, 1960).

[5] *Statistical Abstract of Latin America 1963* (Los Angeles: Center of Latin American Studies, University of California, 1963), p. 76.

[6] A. Chaparro and R. H. Allee, "Higher Agricultural Education and Social Change in Latin America," *Rural Sociology,* XXV (March, 1960), 17.

[7] *Statistical Abstract of Latin America 1963, op. cit.*, p. 29.

[8] *Ibid.*, p. 80.

low wages. . . ."[9] A comparative statement on Costa Rica cannot yet be made on the basis of available data.

Definitions of urbanization vary widely within the region, making really comparable estimates difficult. Both Panama and Costa Rica, however, follow the Latin American and preindustrial pattern of domination of the nation by the capital city. A 1958 estimate of the population of San José was 221,000, or 20.6 per cent of the total population; a 1960 estimate of Panama City placed it at 253,000, or 23.9 per cent of the total population. Both ranked among the first five in Latin America, then, with regard to ratio of size of capital city to total population.[10]

A factor that has been considered by many to be the basis of Costa Rica's relatively democratic political history is the wide distribution of land ownership, the relatively large proportion of small- and medium-size farm proprietors. Recently this characterization of Costa Rican land tenure has come under attack, the varying interpretations being usefully summarized by Busey.[11] He concludes that despite modifications required by recent analyses, Costa Rica still has a relatively wide distribution of land ownership, particularly in comparison with the rest of Central America, as well as selected South American countries for which comparable data are provided. Somewhat surprisingly, he finds "rather equivalent" gross land distribution patterns for Costa Rica and Panama. A further difference between the two, however, seems to lie in the distribution of titles to the land. Busey cites studies showing that as much as 10 per cent of the cultivated land in Costa Rica is held by squatters, that is, in unauthorized form, while a comparable estimate for Panama is 45 per cent. This may be taken as additional evidence of the greater degree of national integration in Costa Rica. Furthermore, it is probable that technical assistance, the provision of credit, and other public and private services to farmers are more likely to be available where the latter have legal title to their lands.

The significance of these brief comparisons of indicators of economic development level and social structure lies in the fact that

---

[9]Harold L. Geisert, *Population Problems in Mexico and Central America* (Washington, D.C.: Population Research Project, George Washington University, 1959), pp. 34-35.

[10]*Statistical Abstract of Latin America 1963, op. cit.*, p. 15.

[11]James L. Busey, *Notes on Costa Rican Democracy* (Boulder: University of Colorado Press, 1962), pp. 62-72.

the two countries are far more similar in these regards than they are different. Despite the differences, they both stand well in advance of the other Central American countries. This suggests that political differences should not be ascribed simply to differences in level of economic development or social structure. This statement of caution seems necessary because Costa Rica has so frequently been described in rather speculative terms as a social and economic paradise in Latin and particularly Central America. This is not to disparage the country in any respect, but it is to say that the character of Costa Rican life compared with Panamanian may be far more a function of politics and political history than of contemporary differences in social structure and economy.

POLITICAL SYSTEMS

Panama can be characterized as politically dominated by a few families whose great wealth is based on commerce and landholdings. The term oligarchy is widely used for these reasons. Though people from socially intermediate and even humble levels have made their way to the top economic and political positions, Panama, despite its substantial number of middle-class citizens, has never experienced anything approaching a middle-class revolution through which the latter have entered the political arena and provided a constant supply of leaders. Public policy has therefore reflected far less *etatisme* than has been the case in countries like Chile, Argentina, Uruguay, and Mexico, through which middle-class interests have been advanced by industrial development projects and programs generally that expand "modern" sectors of the economy and provide large numbers of technical, managerial, and other desirable white-collar jobs. The middle elements have apparently been increasing proportionally, but they have not yet won political status.

There has been a high degree of political competition, but it has been competition based not on ideological differences nor even on political interests, as much as on personal differences and ambitions. The commitment to interests of self, family, and friends has been the primary guide to behavior, in the manner described by Sjoberg as typical of the political culture of the preindustrial society.[12] Corrup-

[12]Gideon Sjoberg, *The Preindustrial City* (Glencoe, Ill.: The Free Press, 1958).

tion and graft are an integral part of the political process, and there seems to be little impetus at present for a radical alteration of these practices. There have been a very large number of political parties, most of them personalist in nature. The only exceptions are the new Christian Democratic party, which has proved ineffective so far in mobilizing even a substantial minority of citizens, and the Panameñista party of twice-president Arnulfo Arias. Panameñismo has stood for a highly diffuse radical nationalism and authoritarianism in the past, but in his 1964 Presidential campaign, from which he emerged the narrow loser amid widespread rumors of systematic distortion of ballot tabulation, Arias' program focused little on nationalism (despite the January riots) and much more on the venality of the oligarchy.

There has therefore been no regularized way in which proponents of change could enter their demands in the political process. Reforms have been enacted by the oligarchy-dominated national assembly, but they have been sporadic and their implementation slight.

Perhaps the public policy status quo has been preservable only because of the pervasive presence of the Yankee. The history of the Canal has provided much stimulus for Panamanian resentment, and for years the Panamanian elite has used the Canal issue to focus popular discontents on foreigners. Rising expectations for a better life and relative stability in the distribution of wealth have stirred ever more inflamed feelings about the Canal. In this context, the successive reforms and concessions made by the United States government to soothe Panamanian hostility have been unsuccessful, as the January, 1964, riots demonstrate. Furthermore, it has become increasingly difficult for the government to control nationalist fervor. It was clear during the recent riots that the government felt constrained from interfering with the violence directed at the Zone, and in the subsequent negotiations with the U.S. government it was clearly able to compromise very little because of the aroused populace and the pressure of the students. It seems fairly certain that demands for nationalization of the Canal will increase, the major ambiguity in the situation being the conjecture about a new canal and its location.

The only Panamanian armed force is the National Guard, whose place in the national power structure is difficult to assess. The Guard has been socially more democratic in its recruitment than have other powerful institutions, but this does not necessarily mean that its interests diverge from those of the traditional elite. The policy status quo has included a constant substantial allocation of values to the Guard, whose officers and men enjoy a relatively high standard of living. Under these conditions, it would be surprising were they to associate themselves politically with elements whose success might threaten their advantageous position in the society. This seems particularly the case so long as oppositionalist elements remain weak and unorganized. Should the latter conditions change, the Guard might well move to monopolize political leadership positions in order to stabilize the political system and protect its perquisites. At this point, there appears to be little affinity between it and any politically reformist elements.

Oligarchy has never seemed to characterize Costa Rica in the degree that it has Panama. Though there is less difference in the extent to which the working class has been integrated into the two political systems, the middle elements clearly are more regular participants in political decision-making in Costa Rica, and the scope of government has been expanded more there than in Panama in a wide variety of state-sponsored economic generative activities.

A great deal of political change has occurred in Costa Rica since 1940. The government of Calderón Guardia was the first to appeal to the urban working class, enacting a good deal of social and welfare state legislation. There was no coherent, comprehensive political organization supporting this government; rather, there was a diffuse coalition of interests including such traditional pillars as large landowners and the church hierarchy, the Communist party, and the personal following of the President, a coalition promoted perhaps by the conditions of international politics during World War II. Calderón's successor continued in his direction, except that the regime grew more dictatorial. Civil liberties were restricted and opponents harassed, and this repression was climaxed by the unconstitutional rejection of the apparently victorious opposition candidate by the *calderonista*-dominated legislature after the 1948 election. A civil war then broke out between the *calderonistas* and Communists on the one side and the insurgent forces of José Figueres, who supported the apparently legally victorious presidential candidate, Otilio Ulate.

An interim period of constitution-writing and consolidation of order followed Figueres' victory. During this time the Communists were proscribed from politics, a capital levy of 10 per cent on the wealthy raised funds to sustain the government, and the banks were nationalized. Stemming from this period is the intense resentment of

Figueres by conservative and traditional elements allied principally with Ulate and in the Partido Unión Nacional, for they may well have expected that the conclusion of the successful fight against *calderonismo* would be not only suppression of the Communists but also the destruction of Costa Rica's fledgling welfare state system, and a return to the traditional scope of government. Instead came an endorsement of the welfare state, the capital levy, the organization of a political party by Figueres aimed at mobilizing some of the very "popular" elements hitherto controlled by the Communists, and alliances with social democrats throughout the region. Despite these sharp differences, Figueres carried through the agreement to turn the government over to Ulate in 1949. Since then, political competition has been three-way, between Figueres' Partido Liberación Nacional, Ulate's PUN, and Calderón's Partido Republicano Nacional. On the whole the latter two have tended to ally against the PLN, which normally appears to be the majority party. The PLN has attempted to attract support from across the social spectrum by emphasizing state-sponsored economic development, the benefits of which will accrue to businessmen, farmers, and urban workers, as well as to expanding managerial and white-collar occupations. This has required moderation in action because of the difficulty of harmonizing so wide a constituency. At the same time, the PLN has been one of the most successful programmatic political parties of Latin America because it has not threatened the establishment to the point of provoking violent countermeasures.[13]

Since the Revolution of 1948, there has been alternation in office without violence through four presidential terms: Figueres to Ulate (PUN) in 1949, Ulate to Figueres (PLN) in 1953, Figueres to Echandi (PUN-PRN coalition) in 1958, and Echandi to Orlich (PLN) in 1962. Thus, though submitted to the test of intense partisanship and hostilities and a recent civil war, Costa Rican constitutionalism has been institutionalized at least throughout this difficult period.

There has been considerable experimentation in Costa Rica with regard to measures designed to strengthen democratic constitutionalism. It is one of the few countries where an OAS neutral team has been invited to observe elections as a guarantee against fraud or rumor of fraud (a frequent aspect of the electoral process in Latin America).

---

[13]On this function of the ideology of the PLN, see Charles Anderson, "Politics and Development Policy in Central America," *Midwest Journal of Political Science,* V (November, 1961), 332-50.

In the same vein, the government defrays a substantial proportion of the election campaign expenses of major parties. Though this has not precluded complaints about violation of electoral laws, it has apparently contributed to a popular climate of confidence in the neutrality of the electoral procedures, which contrasts particularly with the Panamanian experience. There elections have frequently taken place amid widespread expectations of fraud and the result has been occasional violence, frequent cynicism, and an inability of officials to use the election as an indicator of a popular mandate. An exception to this pattern occurred in the 1960 election of an opposition candidate, which contributed to the special significance of the ensuing administration, orientations toward which will be a special concern of this report. The 1964 election, however, took place amid the same expectations and climate of fraud.

While Panama's problematic foreign relations have been with the United States, Costa Rica has been far more embroiled in intra-Latin American politics. Figueres and other PLN leaders have maintained close relations with such prominent social democratic leaders as Betancourt, Muñoz Marín, and Bosch. During the time the PLN has held the presidency, Costa Rica has received social democratic exiles cordially, creating hostile relations with dictatorial governments, such as those of Somoza, Trujillo, and Pérez Jiménez. Other Costa Rican leaders have resented the difficulties this policy has provoked. The most serious problems arose with northern neighbor Nicaragua during the last years of the old dictator Somoza's rule, when that country served as a haven and rallying point for the *calderonistas.* An invasion from Nicaragua led to the effective intervention of an OAS peacekeeping mission in 1955. These hostilities have made far more difficult the development of Central American cooperation in economic and political activities, though there are indications of a diminishing intensity of the conflict.

Costa Rican relations with the United States have tended to be positive and relatively unemotional. A traditional point of sensitivity, the role of the United Fruit Company, has declined in salience since Figueres' successful renegotiation of the Company's contract in 1954, in which agreement was reached to double the tax rate, among other changes. These agreements became models for future United Fruit-Central American government contracts.

Since the revolution of 1948, the nature of the military establishment has been radically changed: following the defeat of the regular forces by the insurgents, the decision was made to dissolve the army and rely on a minimally manned civil guard. Since that time, the country has spent very little money on its armed force, relying principally on the OAS, the United States, and emergency volunteers for defense purposes. In comparison with the military in Panama, and in most Latin American countries, the Costa Rican military is not a major element of the power structure.

No primary research reports are available to provide a basis for comparing the manner of government functioning in the two countries. For example, there are low-cost public housing and social security programs in both countries, but their extent and effectiveness cannot be assessed here. Costa Rica appears to have made an earlier start on programs designed to meet the problems of the urban poor; an example is the minimum wage law, enacted in 1954 in Costa Rica and in 1959 in Panama. The gap between written provisions and effective implementation is so characteristic of Latin American social legislation, however, that no conclusions can be drawn from such crude facts.

PROBLEMS OF ECONOMIC DEVELOPMENT AND SOCIAL REFORM: COSTA RICA

Further expansion of the scope of government in social and welfare areas faces great barriers in the two countries, though the nature of the barriers is substantially different. In Costa Rica's case, a decline in the price of coffee has sharply diminished the revenues available to the government and demonstrated the generally precarious position in international trade of a country which depends heavily on a few agricultural exports which are also produced by a large number of competitors. For example, taking 1958 as a base year (the 1958 price index equals 100), the Costa Rican price index for exports dropped from 120 in 1957 to 72 in 1962, while the price index for imports slightly increased, from 100 to 103, over the same period. Comparative figures for Panama show the same but much less drastic trend, the export price index declining from 103 to 87, while the import index varied exactly as Costa Rica's.[14] The adverse trend for Panama was also softened by the fact that it depends much more on Zone activities and purchases, which steadily increased, at least until the January, 1964, riots, than on exports.

In addition, the prolonged ash eruptions of the volcano Irazú

[14]*Statistical Abstract of Latin America 1963, op. cit.*, p. 111.

destroyed farm land and products and cost the government heavily in disasters such as floods and in emergency measures for keeping the streets of the capital cleared of debris. As a result, the Orlich (PLN) government found itself not only prevented from making good on campaign promises for economic expansion and extended welfare programs, but at times financially incapable of meeting the cost of current programs such as the payment of public hospital costs, of rapidly growing demands on basic public services such as the provision of water, even in the metropolitan area of the capital, and at times unable even to meet the payroll deadline for public employees or to grant now-traditional Christmas bonuses. The government was at times so poor that it was unable to meet its share of the cost of a number of Alliance for Progress projects, the pace of which therefore slowed, provoking some resentment on the part of public officials. They believe that Costa Rican efforts to meet social problems much preceded those of other Latin American countries and the Alliance, and that their current problems justified greater allowance.

One area in which there has been a recent significant shift in the scope of government concerns Central American cooperation. The Echandi government had rejected Costa Rican membership in the Central American Common Market, reflecting its own conservative orientation toward political economy and the traditional Costa Rican attitude of superiority toward its neighbors. The Orlich government reversed that position, not only becoming a member of the organization but a strong promoter of regionally oriented commercial and industrial expansion. So far, the success of the market has been substantial.

There seems little impetus at the present time toward reformation of the tax structure in a more progressive direction, an action that would provide more funds for meeting the growing social problems. These are in considerable degree a function of the relationship between the economic decline and a rate of population growth that is the highest in Latin America and one of the very highest in the world —averaging 4.4 per cent annually for the period 1958-1961, compared with 2.7 per cent for Panama.[15] Since there also seems to have been a relationship in recent Costa Rican history between progressive policies and periods of economic expansion, such impetus for shifts in the scope of government may await a reversal of the current economic condition.

[15] *Ibid.*, p. 17.

In any event, the economic decline and the resultant contraction in the scope of government, after the raising and reinforcing of high expectations for a better life by PLN propaganda, may be sorely felt in Costa Rica, for it follows a decade of substantial economic growth and expanding government. From 1946 to 1956 total real gross national product grew by 7.1 per cent, much faster than the population, so that there were annual per capita gains of 3.8 per cent. During this same period in Panama, real gross national product in relation to population "either failed to keep pace or dropped slightly behind."[16]

PROBLEMS OF ECONOMIC DEVELOPMENT AND SOCIAL REFORM: PANAMA

THE ELECTION OF 1960 AND THE CHIARI ADMINISTRATION

The May, 1960, election resulted surprisingly in victory for one of the opposition Presidential candidates, Roberto Chiari. Such an event was virtually unprecedented, and a special tranquillity lasted through the transfer of office in October. There was therefore an ambience of democratic constitutionalism, and the administration could lay claim, far more than its predecessors, to a popular mandate.

This four-year Presidential term reflected many of the most fundamental political pressures and weaknesses that characterize Latin America generally, and they coincided with the most comprehensive program ever undertaken by the United States to resolve its outstanding differences with the countries of the region and to develop new relations based on mutual interest. For these reasons, and because of the aforementioned set of attitudinal data available, the Chiari administration will be subjected to special scrutiny in this report.

Chiari assumed office at a time when *fidelismo* was strong and still ascending as a Latin American political movement. Cuban events engrossed a great many Panamanians, particularly those among the intellectual sectors, an attraction probably based on the significant similarities in Cuban and Panamanian political history. For example, both were newly independent nations relative to other Latin American countries (Cuban independence came in 1898, Panamanian in 1903), and the United States was involved in imperialist fashion at both birth rites. The U.S. remained the dominant foreign relation in both cases,

[16]Louis J. Ducoff, *Human Resources of Central America, Panama, and Mexico 1950-1980, in Relation to Some Aspects of Economic Development* (Mexico: United Nations Economic Commission for Latin America, 1960), p. 81.

intervening directly in domestic politics, often at the request of the domestic government. The degree of intervention declined markedly over the years, but the legacy of resentment augmented. U.S. sugar, mining, cattle, and utility interests played a major role in the Cuban economy; these were matched by the role of the Canal and the United Fruit Company in Panama. Both nations have been characterized by extreme economic dependence on the United States, widespread poverty, unemployment, and extreme political corruption. One of the reactions to domestic inadequacy and quasi-colonial status has been virulent Panamanian and Cuban nationalism.

In Cuba the 1940's was a time of testing whether constitutional democracy as a political regime was adequate to the task of economic and social transformation and the creation of a viable degree of political legitimacy. The failure of the major political parties was followed by a resumption of the Batista dictatorship and the *fidelista* social revolution. In Panama, a counterpart test of constitutional democracy may have occurred during the Chiari presidency.

Chiari himself called attention to this. While Castro inveighed against the Panamanian oligarchy and urged the people to rise up, destroy the system, and nationalize the Canal, the new President pronounced himself an oligarch, probably the last of that small circle to hold the Presidency, and declared against *fidelismo* and communism. He advocated social reform and economic development by persuasion. Addressing the power elite of the country, he predicted that change was inevitable and near, and that a failure at reform would be succeeded by events paralleling those in Cuba. As local *fidelista* activity was suppressed and Cuban-Panamanian relations virtually severed, Chiari relied increasingly on the able U.S. ambassador to dampen the hostilities fired by the riots on the Zone border on Panamanian Independence Day, November 3, 1959. (The most violent in Isthmian history, they had been put down by U.S. armed force, with no deaths.) The Kennedy promulgation of the Alliance for Progress reinforced his early efforts to ease the reform and development process by reliance on massive U.S. financial and technical assistance. The latter was forthcoming, and projects were begun in low-cost housing, school, and public health center construction, etc., most of which were designed to have an early, tangible impact on the people.

The political structure, however, remained the same. Chiari had been elected at the head of a coalition of parties, all of them personalist, and no efforts were made during his administration to develop a political organization capable of mobilizing citizens behind a program. This was all the more important because the Presidential term is short —four years—and the incumbent may not immediately seek re-election, so that continuity in policy required organization. Despite executive expressions about reform and development, the National Assembly delayed and deterred shifts in the scope of government designed to promote those ends. Minor tax reforms were made, and an agrarian reform law was passed, but enforcement as of mid-1964 was slight.

The Alliance for Progress languished in this environment. It had, of course, been proposed by the Kennedy administration as a concerted attempt to enlist the cooperation of Latin Americans in the task of altering their societies so as to produce the substance for a much higher standard of living and to distribute this substance in a manner that was sufficiently egalitarian to produce that higher standard of living for the total population. The program had signified the assumption by the U.S. government, after roughly a decade of argument by Latin American intellectual reformists, that constitutional democracy and commitment to "open societies" is likely to occur only in association with widespread popular faith in the effectiveness of government and society. The Alliance asked Latin Americans to use U.S. assistance to effect a comprehensive social transformation, by means of persuasion, while maintaining a stable economic climate attractive to foreign and domestic private investment. It required the Latin Americans to work with, and essentially under the direction of, the United States, certainly in foreign policy, despite the history of Latin American-U.S. hostilities and increasingly intense nationalism. Approximately three years after the inception of the Alliance, substantial and varying evaluations have appeared; many of these find the program not only deviating from and falling short of its projected goals, but, far more seriously, lacking the environment of commitment, without which other resources such as money and goods cannot make significant contributions to the program.[17] Most criticism holds that the

[17]Some useful evaluations include Victor Alba, "Parásitos, Mitos y Sordomudos," supplement to *Panoramas* (septiembre-octubre, 1964), Tad Szulc, *The Winds of Revolution* (New York: Praeger, 1965); Simon Hanson, "The Alliance for Progress: The Third Year," *Inter-American Economic Affairs,* XVIII (Spring, 1965); Peter Nehemkis, *Latin America; Myth and Reality* (New York: Knopf, 1964); and Claudio Veliz, "Obstacles to Reform in Latin America," *The World Today,* XIX (January, 1963). For an analysis of U.S.-Latin American ideological differences on matters of political economy, see John P. Powelson, *Latin America: Today's Economic and Social Revolution* (New York: McGraw-Hill, 1964); and Frederick B. Pike, *Chile and the United States: 1880-1962* (Notre Dame: University of Notre Dame Press, 1963).

prevailing elites in Latin America lack the commitment to, or are committed against, basic change. This being the case, the other criticisms, such as lack of policy coordination among U.S. agencies, seem trivial.

The Panamanian experience with the Alliance bears out many of these general observations. In the absence of organized political commitment and greatly augmented public financial resources, Alliance projects made relatively little progress. The Panamanian official in charge of the development program announced in October, 1963, that only one-third of the funds made available by the Alliance had been spent. "Of 2.9 million for agriculture, 3 for a water system, and 4 for electrification, only 85,000, 332,000, and 146,000 respectively had been disbursed."[18] Even a 9.9 million dollar grant from President Kennedy's contingency fund for "key projects in Panama's five-year investment program" was expended at the same slow rate.[19] U.S. responsibility for failures appeared to include lack of coordination of agencies responsible for various aspects of the Alliance, and a fiasco on an originally low-cost housing project that became an upper-middle income development, involving unusual secret negotiations, special senatorial pressures in behalf of an interested party to the project, exclusion of competition, etc.[20] These contributions to the low level of performance of the Alliance loomed small compared with those of the Panamanian government. For example, the same report found "a decided lack of enthusiasm at official government levels for expansion of industrial activities." Social development projects were delayed or dropped because the governmental organizations involved were inadequate. Governmental revenues were too restricted even to meet existing public works responsibilities, let alone new social development projects, and interest and amortization payments on the latter accentuated the deficit problems. The housing institute, for example, was so short of funds that it could not provide "urbanization" (streets, lights, sewers) for the housing involved in Alliance projects. As if to indicate positive harassment of the endeavor, the report mentioned the Panamanian government's levying commodity import taxes (now

[18]*Hispanic American Report,* XVI (December, 1963), 958.

[19]Report of the Staff Survey Team of the Subcommittee for Review of the Mutual Security Programs of the House Committee on Foreign Affairs, *The Housing Investment Guaranty Program and the Economic Aid Program in Panama* (Washington, D.C.: Government Printing Office, November 19, 1963), p. 5.

[20]*Ibid.*; and E. W. Kenworthy, "Report Critical on Aid to Panama," *New York Times* (Western Edition), December 19, 1963, p. 3.

discontinued) on materials brought in for construction of schools, health facilities, and agricultural stations.

Another promising aspect of Panamanian-United States relations had been the formation of bi-national teams to work out modifications of the Canal treaty to both parties' satisfaction. Progress had been slow here too, however, and the opportunity appeared to have been lost with the January, 1964, riots, which far surpassed any preceding outbreak in violence, deaths, and national resentment on both sides. Both governments subsequently found concessions difficult to make.

The January violence marked at least a temporary reversal of an economic trend, and this threatened to aggravate much more deeply the problems associated with political stagnation and defensive nationalism. Since the late 1950's, the Panamanian gross national product had been expanding at a rapid rate. If economic expansion had generated high expectations for a better life among Panamanians, the riots had caused an immediate decline of substantial proportions that could only have disappointed such expectations. It is of course too early to conclude what the long-range effects of these events will be. At this point in time, however, it seems useful to cite James C. Davies' hypothesis that revolutions tend to occur where economic expansion has bred high hopes, only to be followed by an abrupt, and therefore acutely frustrating, decline.[21]

Thus, both Costa Rica and Panama have had national experiences recently that would seem to occasion considerable and widespread discontent. Much depends on the existence of a "cushion" of political legitimacy in the two countries, and it is to that problem that this study is directed.

---

[21]"Toward a Theory of Revolution," *American Sociological Review,* XXVII (February, 1962), 5-19.

CHAPTER IV

POLITICAL PROFILES: TIME 1

THIS CHAPTER PROVIDES THE BASE LINE FOR THE SUBSEQUENT analysis. It presents a profile of the political orientations of the Panamanian and Costa Rican students at Time 1, that is, 1961 in Panama and 1962 in Costa Rica. Subsequently, in Chapter V, change and stasis in Panamanian orientations are examined for the period Time 1 to Time 2, 1961-1963, and the "mood" of the Panamanians at Time 2 will then be assessed again in comparison with that of the Costa Ricans (who were studied only in 1962). A graphic description of the comparisons that will be made is given below:

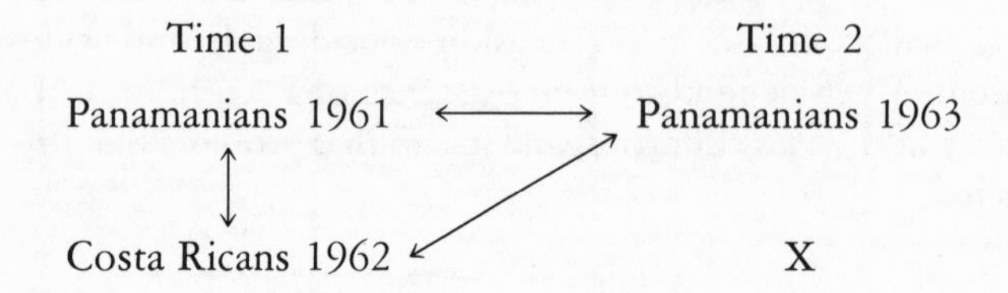

EIGHT TYPES OF ORIENTATION

Data on eight types of orientations are presented and analyzed. In addition to politicization and legitimacy orientations, the rationale for which has been given in the introductory chapter, six other orientational dimensions are used to organize the analysis because they seem to be critical in the political psychology of actors seeking political change. These other dimensions include: expectations for personal success; expectations about others' chances; positions on specific domestic policy changes; evaluation of the nation's position vis-à-vis other nations, particularly traditionally superordinate nations and contemporary challengers of the traditionally dominant; beliefs about the effectiveness of various means in politics; and evaluations of the latter. The eight dimensions are briefly elaborated in their order of presentation.

EXPECTATIONS ABOUT PERSONAL SUCCESS

Frustrated aspirations for success in life are widely considered to have important political consequences. Particularly in the case of intellectuals in societies in transition from preindustrialism, frustration over lack of opportunity has been proposed as a key factor in generating intense politicization and oppositionalism.[1] By inference, the expectation of success is assumed to promote support for the system and something less than intense politicization. This, however, overlooks frustration arising from deprivation of values other than wealth and status, such as rectitude, involving a sense of shame about the condition of the nation, aside from personal prospects for success. For example, Cuban upper-status youth turned strongly to Castro against Batista, despite an expanding economy and prospects for their socioeconomic success, at least partly because of their strong sense of shame at the corruption, brutality, and immorality of national political life.[2] Privileged youth in the Dominican Republic, with the example of Castro before them, have been described as having turned against Trujillo at tremendous personal cost for many of the same reasons, despite the fact that their fathers had benefited substantially from his rule and despite their own prospects for continuing that pattern.[3] Kecskemeti has described the key role of the Party writers, a relatively highly privileged group, in triggering the Hungarian Revolution of 1956. Their behavior is seen as a function of their profound sense of shame, following Khrushchev's denunciation of Stalin, at their having glorified such a tyranny.[4] Political opposition, despite high expectations of personal success, will be treated as an important empirical possibility in the following analysis.

---

[1]E. Shils, "Intellectuals in the Political Development of the New States," *World Politics,* XII (April, 1960), 329-68.

[2]On the role of shame as a motivation for rebellion in Cuba, see F. G. Gil, "Some Antecedents of the Cuban Revolution," *The Centennial Review,* VI (Summer, 1962), 373-93.

[3]Juan Bosch, "Crisis de la Democracia de América en la República Dominicana," Suplemento a la Revista *Panoramas,* No. 14 (marzo-abril, 1965); published in English as *The Unfinished Experiment: Democracy in the Dominican Republic* (New York: Praeger, 1965).

[4]*The Unexpected Revolution* (Stanford: Stanford University Press, 1961), p. 117.

BELIEFS ABOUT OTHERS' CHANCES FOR SUCCESS

With regard to upper-status Latin American students our concern is the extent to which personal advantages and bases of influence are perceived against a backdrop of generally severe limitations on social and political mobility and a highly unequal distribution of wealth, status, and power. When someone's aspirations are blocked, it is not surprising to find his personal frustration producing a strong identification with large masses of people perceived as similarly deprived (unjustly), and his taking part in a broad-scale attack on privilege in the name of the downtrodden. But if his personal expectations are high, it requires an unusual perspective – seeing others' problems before their grievances become so intense that they undermine one's own position in the society. If others' problems are perceived – if, for example, there is agreement that the social situation of the deprived is a problem – then there are greater possibilities for a political conversation between elites and representatives of the deprived. Persistent denial that such problems exist has led to the progressive incapacity of some old elites to accommodate grievances before the protest grew too intense to control. Crozier has written on variations in the development of postwar insurrectionary movements as a function of variation in the timing of the elite's redefinition of a traditional social situation as problematic.[5]

POLITICIZATION

The level of politicization must be assessed to validate for this group the widespread belief that Latin American students are keenly aware of and involved in politics. Some variation in the phenomenon is to be expected. Is this high salience of politics lacking among the sons of the establishment, perhaps because they take for granted a future controlling role in the national polity? Or is political awareness more highly developed among the Costa Rican than the Panamanian representatives of this stratum as a result of the less oligarchic politics of the former country? Variation in types of politicization may also be contingent on the sense of deprivation and the environment of these upper-status students. That is, sons of the elite who feel uncertain of their own future or ashamed of the living conditions of the populace may feel strongly inhibited from talking about it within the establish-

[5]*The Rebels: A Study of Postwar Insurrections* (Boston: Beacon Press, 1960).

ment ambience for fear of the stigma of class disloyalty. Their discussion rates may be low, while their perception of the relevance of government may be extremely high.

LEGITIMACY

The central concern of this report is the students' evaluation of the political system, of politicians, and the political process.

SPECIFIC POSITIONS ON REFORM

Ambivalence or opposition to the political system may be a function of intensely felt needs for reform. But it is of major importance whether the program of reform priorities is shared among dissidents. If they are disunited in their view of what needs doing, even a large sector of dissidents may be unable to bring about basic changes in the system, and even an overwhelmingly illegitimate political system may persist. If they are united, there is a greater probability of change.

NATIONALISM, NEUTRALISM, COMMUNISM

Since relations between the national political system and other political systems are crucial in contemporary politics, as, for example, where nationalist movements destroy former colonial or quasi-colonial ties and provide through independence the base of legitimacy for a new political system, orientations toward nationalism, neutralism, the United States, and communism all bear inquiry. Where resentment of second-class status or dependence on another nation is intense, domestic policies may be lacking in salience, as citizens focus on the diffuse, pervasive matter of the status of the nation.[6] Incumbent elites too closely identified with the interests of the traditionally dominant foreign nation may bring about rapid loss of system legitimacy and ascendant, assertive politicization among a normally acquiescent, non-politicized citizenry. Among youth affiliated with the old elite, sympathy for the nationalist cause may over time contribute to the demoralization of the old elite. However, contemporary nationalism everywhere in the transitional world has become identified and

---

[6]See Frank Bonilla's analysis of Brazilian nationalism relative to this point in K. H. Silvert (ed.), *Expectant Peoples* (New York: Random House, 1963), pp. 232-64.

involved with an international movement toward "independence" on the part of the poor, essentially colored nations. Upper-status Latin American youth may be unable to identify very strongly with this alien, "crude" form of the new nationalism, and thus to the extent that radical nationalists from lower social strata look outward for support of their movement, the active local support of such upper-status youth may be limited.

BELIEFS ABOUT THE EFFECTIVENESS OF VARIOUS MEANS

Given the goals, given the tensions that motivate political behavior, how effective are a range of political means perceived to be? Specifically, the focus is on the perceived effectiveness of regular channels, slightly irregular practices, and revolutionary ones. Despite opposition to the existing system, some people continue to accept as effective means to political change that are probably incapable of bringing it about.

PREFERENCES FOR VARIOUS POLITICAL MEANS

Given perceptions of the effectiveness of alternative means, which of them are preferred, and how are preferences ranked? A contemporary syndrome of orientations in Latin America among the relatively privileged may well combine perception of social problems, ambivalence about the system, support for reforms, perception of "normal" means as ineffective in implementing these reforms, but abhorrence of or extreme hesitancy regarding revolutionary means. Such a syndrome suggests a condition of political immobilism.

No hypotheses are developed at this point about the nature of the profiles under investigation. The orientation of Latin American students has received so little systematic attention that guidelines are indistinct and contradictory. For example, the Panamanian system has been described as relatively static, with an oligarchy of long duration challenged only by diffuse, potential competition, despite the fact of widespread and increasing dissatisfaction among the citizens. What then is the political mood of those who stand in direct line of political inheritance? They can be any of the following: unaware, uncaring, uncritical, exponents of the status quo which so (relatively) richly rewards them now and which they may take for granted will continue to do so; jealous of their privileges and discontented with a system that seems to have allowed at least inchoate disaffection among the underdogs; deeply committed to the good life made possible and protected by such a system, and yet ambivalent about the condition of the poor as a result of their youthful decency and idealism; or fed up with age-old exploitation and ready to go over to a radically different system of producing and allocating values, regardless of the manner in which it would change their own lives. Of Costa Rica, paragon of decency, democracy, and egalitarianism in Latin America according to foreign observers, so little is known that one can expect any of several political moods among the sons of well-placed families there too: a restorationist syndrome associated with lingering resentment of the changes toward a modern welfare-state system established by the revolution of 1948 and the Figueres forces; acceptance of these changes and the new or modified political system; or ambivalence, combining resentment toward the authors of recent change but neutrality, acquiescence, or even support for the policy changes themselves. Where so many alternatives are "reasonable," the best initial course of action seems to me the undertaking of a descriptive profile of orientations.

ORIENTATION PROFILES

EXPECTATIONS ABOUT PERSONAL SUCCESS (TABLE A-1)[7]

Both student groups seemed highly confident about their future position in society. Despite the different pressures for social change in the two countries, there were no differences between Costa Ricans and Panamanians in their expectations for personal success. Half of them strongly affirmed the proposition, "I will get the job I deserve," and 80 per cent reported at least substantial agreement with it.[8] Only about 1 in 20 indicated any measure of agreement with the statement, "I will never attain the success I want." Asked to compare themselves with other students in their school regarding their assessment of

[7]The tables for this chapter are found in Appendix A, pp. 103-13, and are referred to in the heading of each of the following sections dealing with an orientational dimension as Table A-1 through Table A-8.

[8]The item referred to here is of the "agree-disagree" type used to collect much of the data on which the study was based. The item consists in a proposition about which the respondent is asked to indicate his extent of agreement or disagreement, ranging from strong through substantial to slight agreement, and slight through substantial to strong disagreement.

future success, one-fourth saw themselves among "those on top," while another one-half saw themselves doing "very well," with most of the remainder saying they would do merely "well." Only a very small minority agreed strongly or substantially with the proposition that "Only if things change very much will I attain the success I want," and more than two-thirds disagreed with it.

If general success seems assured to the students, political power appears to be regarded as more problematical. Though only a very few indicated strong agreement that "Only if things change very much will I attain the political influence I want," over half expressed some degree of agreement with it. But this suggests that potential discontent with one's personal political influence is not directly related to or a function of frustration over general success in life. (This will be more directly assessed in Chapter VI.) And whether the "changes" required before political influence can be attained involve major or minor modifications of the political system will be assessed below.

BELIEFS ABOUT OTHERS' CHANCES FOR SUCCESS (TABLE A-2)

The students' beliefs about the general availability of opportunity in their country were much more varied than were their expectations for personal success. Over half agreed strongly that "One can succeed in this country with ability and effort," and there was hardly anyone who did not agree in some measure. The following, more specific question was also designed to tap belief in the openness of the opportunity system: "What is the most important for success in this country: hard work, skill, family position, or money?" A response of "hard work" and "skill" reflects a belief in openness and achievement as the major means of success. A majority of both groups, somewhat larger among the Costa Ricans, selected one or other of these alternatives, but this is a considerable decline in the perception of openness from that suggested by the almost completely affirmative response to the more general preceding question.

Furthermore, a preponderance, substantially larger among the Panamanians, held that "The majority of the good things in life are controlled by the few." This suggests that responses to the first item reflect a belief that while it is *possible for an individual* to succeed, etc., on the whole, values are rather narrowly distributed.

Another indicator of the quality of social insights is the perception of the limitation on opportunity according to color. Only a minority of the Panamanians and even fewer of the Costa Ricans saw racial discrimination as a possible block to success. This minority rejected the proposition that "There is no racial discrimination in this country." With regard to colored citizens in the two countries, it seems that the students were cognitively far removed from their condition. Though even less perceptive than the Panamanians in this regard, the Costa Ricans are probably more fortunate, in that their racial problem is of smaller dimensions: their colored citizens are less angry than the Panamanians' and much less dangerously situated in a geographic sense, living predominantly in the coastal areas of low politicization.

It appears, then, that in general more of the two groups of students see others' chances for success as more problematical than they do their own. In view of the prevailing image of difference between the two societies, the relative similarity in the pattern of beliefs of the two groups is surprising, even though a fairly consistent small difference in the expected direction did occur.

When the focus is narrowed to the matter of success in politics, a much sharper difference appears. It is assumed that either of the first two responses to the following question indicates a belief in the openness of the political system: "What is most important for political success in this country: hard work, political program, family position, or money?" Only half of the Panamanians selected either one of the first two, compared with four-fifths of the Costa Ricans, with the greatest difference occurring in mentions of "political program." In that relatively programmatic parties are operative in Costa Rica while none are in Panama, the great difference in belief accords with the facts. The recognition by a large proportion of these high-status Panamanians that there are severe social structural limitations on political mobility in their country is at least potentially important. Recognition of this situation places them some distance closer to the wide range of reformist opinion in their country holding that political opportunity is limited to the few. A denial by the well-off that this is the situation would render it more difficult to begin a political conversation since the "facts" of the protagonists would differ.

POLITICIZATION (TABLE A-3)

There are several alternative hypotheses readily available to predict the pattern of politicization of sons of the establishment. The amount of politicization may be low, particularly in Panama, because the shape of the world is taken for granted and the impulse to political awareness is consequently missing. In Costa Rica, politics involves more controversy over policy alternatives, and the privileged are engaged in politics as but one set of participants among many, and therefore the general political environment may serve to politicize these students. On the other hand, the ferment of the past half-decade generated by the Cuban Revolution and a rise in locally articulated discontents may be hypothesized as sufficient to have created a threat to these Panamanians' inheritance of elite positions, with the result that politicization will now be high. Another obvious hypothesis is that both student groups will be highly politicized simply as a function of being brought up in a family atmosphere highly charged with national political involvement.

It has been noted above that both sets of students showed a high level of confidence about their personal chances for success. Thus the hypothesis postulating a reaction to class threat seems incongruous, at least without taking into account further conditions. And the first one, as it turns out, fits rather poorly as well. Though it is impossible in any complete sense to judge levels of politicization without comparing students of this high social background with, for example, others below them, it is possible to show that very few choose to characterize themselves as having a low level of awareness and involvement. For example, although about half of each group agrees that "What any government does will not affect my life very much," only 25 per cent of the Panamanians and 13 per cent of the Costa Ricans expressed "no interest" in politics, and 38 and 47 per cent respectively described their interest as at least substantial. Although only a minority of one-fifth in both groups had a present intention of "going into" politics upon completion of education, only 15 per cent of the Panamanians and 10 per cent of the Costa Ricans said they "never discuss" politics with their school friends, compared with more than one-third who said they do so "frequently," and only about one-fourth reported no discussion with family or with non-school friends. Fully three-fifths of the Panamanians and half the Costa Ricans reported frequent discussion of the Cuban Revolution, while the merest 1 per cent of each said they have never discussed it. With regard to attendance at meetings related to the previous national elections, half the Costa Ricans and just under a third of the Panamanians reported participation, a finding that corresponds with our earlier characterization of the difference in the importance of partisan activities in the two countries. Finally, even though the very well-situated high school student is not noted in either country for his participation in "typical" student politicking, less than one-third of the Panamanians and one-fifth of the Costa Ricans reported no participation in any student "demonstrations." Thus the conclusion appears warranted that large segments of both sets of students reflect a relatively high level of politicization and a very small segment reflects a low level. In combination with their expression of confidence about their personal future success, which finding seems to rule out the "threat" hypothesis's applicability, the evidence does not conflict with the socialization hypothesis that the close relation of their parents to politics has served to politicize the sons as well.[9]

Had the level of politicization of either group been extremely low, it would have suggested that the following presentation of data on political legitimacy, reformism, etc. had been affected. That is, a low degree of salience of politics might be assumed to produce substantive political opinions of a very tentative nature which bear little relation to present or future behavior.

EVALUATION OF THE POLITICAL SYSTEM (TABLE A-4)

In general, the questionnaire used in Panama at Time 1 (1961) was particularly inadequate with regard to the range of items tapping evaluation of the regime, whereas it elicited much more information on decision-makers. This condition was changed in succeeding research, so that the second Panamanian set of data and the Costa Rican data are both more adequate in measuring legitimacy orientations. Nonetheless, with what is available from the 1961 study on this dimension, a base line can be established and change analyzed.

A general item evaluative of the political system asks whether "Government and politics are good for the country, bad, or neither one nor the other." At this level, there is no difference between Panamanians and Costa Ricans; little over half of each responded affirmatively, and less than one-fifth negatively. A companion item, focusing on the political process more specifically, asked whether "Politics and government are honest, dishonest, or neither." Similarity is more remarkable than difference here, with the majority responding "neither," and one-fifth saying "dishonest" in Panama, compared with

[9]It should be stated that the evidence would fit any general socialization hypothesis, in the sense that the data presented do not isolate specific socializing (politicizing) agents.

about one-tenth in Costa Rica. So far, then, the emerging pattern suggests a weighting in both groups between support and either ambivalence or neutrality.

An item that suggested, though only indirectly, evaluation of the rules of the game asked partisan affiliation or identification: "With what party are you affiliated?" The concern here is not specific partisanship, but whether or not the whole electoral-parliamentary system of decision-making has sufficient value for the students to have won their affiliation and therefore at least partial integration into the system. The Panamanians were much less integrated in this sense, for only slightly more than half reported affiliation with any party, compared with four-fifths of the Costa Ricans.

Since all of the existing parties in Panama are controlled by various leaders identified with the prevailing elite and differ virtually not at all in their programs, it matters little for present purposes with which particular parties the half of the students are affiliated. The pattern of affiliations of the Costa Ricans, however, is instructive. Of the 79 per cent who were self-identified partisans, only 14 per cent were supporters of the PRN, the most personalistic of the three major parties, the leading supporters of which traditionally have been stanchly conservative landowners and the Communists, but which attracted considerable lower-class support under former President Calderón Guardia. Slightly more of the students, 21 per cent, supported the PUN, a less personalistic and more programmatic conservative party. The largest grouping, 43 per cent, were partisans of the PLN, the moderate welfare-statist organization begun by José Figueres, the country's largest party, and that against which conservatives have rallied since the Revolution of 1948.

This indicates that the party of the Revolution, the PLN, has been substantially successful in aggregating interests on other than a class basis, so that politics does not represent a constant "showdown" between the socially deprived and the privileged. Additional evidence shows that this socially integrative recruitment began with the fathers of the students surveyed here, because the pattern of their party affiliations (as reported by their sons) is similar to their own, except that the PUN and PRN have somewhat more support among the fathers. The students' reports of their friends' affiliations, however, is far different: the PLN is supported by 65 per cent, the PUN by 8 per cent, and the PRN by 10 per cent. Thus, over time, the PLN appears to be recruiting a much larger proportion of the establishment, which suggests the possibility that the national political integration problems of the future may be generated within that party, as the range of interests it aggregates expands, rather than between it and its older and weaker competitors.

Party orientations are relevant in another respect. The Costa Rican students were asked the degree to which they approved, disapproved, or felt indifferent toward each of the parties. The pattern of evaluations follows generally the pattern of affiliations, but what is significant is the infrequence of strongly disapproving attitudes toward any of the major parties. Nor is this simply a function of lack of enthusiasm for any of the parties; the PLN was strongly approved by 37 per cent (compared with 17 per cent for the PUN and 8 per cent for the PRN), but the most widely disapproved, the PRN, was strongly disapproved by only 13 per cent. The presence of a substantial minority of strong party adherents plus the absence of any substantial number of strong antagonists would indicate another element of high political integration, insofar as the upper-status students are concerned.

A focus on decision-makers also shows large inter-national differences. Sixty-four per cent of the Panamanians rejected the statement, "The majority of public officials work in behalf of the public welfare," compared with 37 per cent of the Costa Ricans. Asked whether "A great many politicians sell themselves easily," half the Panamanians and only 25 per cent of the Costa Ricans agreed strongly, 77 per cent of the Panamanians agreed at least substantially, as did 39 per cent of the Costa Ricans, and fully 90 per cent of the Panamanians agreed in some measure, in contrast with 61 per cent of the Costa Ricans.

What emerges then is a picture of the Panamanians as by no means absolutely alienated from their political system, but not integrated institutionally into it, and highly negative toward politicians as a whole. By comparison the Costa Ricans are highly integrated through the party system, less cynical and much more positive about their politicians as a whole.

In this context, one of the very few strengths of the Panamanian political system vis-à-vis the sons of the establishment was their evaluation of the President, Chiari. Thirty-eight per cent of them strongly approved of him, and 87 per cent approved in some measure, with only 4 per cent reporting disapproval. (A third disapproved of his predecessor, and less than one-half approved of him.) By comparison, the Costa Ricans showed overwhelming approval of their incumbent

President, Orlich, but the amount and the intensity of approval was less. Furthermore, they evaluated his predecessor, representing a different and ideologically opposed party, in identical fashion. This suggests the possibly critical position of Chiari in the politics of legitimacy in Panama, where the party system has substantially failed to integrate even the sons of the well-off who gain so much by that system, and where politicians as a whole are the object of intense disapproval and cynicism. By contrast, the Costa Rican system appears sufficiently legitimate in the eyes of the sons of the establishment (despite the tendencies toward redistribution of wealth since the *figuerista* revolution of 1948) not to "need" highly popular Presidents, and yet its current and preceding chief executives are both objects of positive feeling among a large majority, despite their outstanding partisan and policy differences.

But Chiari's socially reformist and politically democratic stance was highly ambiguous. It is quite possible that his reformism may have been taken by some among the elite as a necessary strategy to absorb the discontent waxing in the country but not as an indicator of serious intentions to restructure the society. To others among the elite, his position may have meant just what his words said—that reforms are a matter of simple justice, long overdue. An inquiry into orientations toward reform, then, should make clearer the meaning of Chiari's Presidency during this critical period of Panamanian history.

POSITION ON SOME REFORM ISSUES (TABLE A-5)

Although many of the powerful people in Latin America oppose welfare state policies, there is strong support for an integral part of this welfare system among the privileged students, at least on the verbal level. Considering the proposition that "The government should provide work to everyone who needs it," over half of both samples indicated strong agreement, and almost none rejected it. Serious agrarian problems exist in both countries; they differ in that Costa Rica has a pattern of more widespread land ownership, and in that country's having made some initial steps at public acquisition of large holdings for distribution to workers located on them, and in the prevailing and pervasive influence of a very few major landowners in Panama. Apparently many of these Panamanian students believe that land reform is a problem. In response to the statement, "This country needs a major agrarian reform," 41 per cent of them and 25 per cent of the Costa Ricans agreed strongly, and the vast majority agreed with less intensity to the proposition. On the more specific matter of financing reform according to ability to pay, however, there was less over-all agreement and less intense agreement. Asked whether "The rich should pay much higher taxes than they now do," half or more agreed in some measure, but only one-fourth to one-fifth agreed strongly. This indicates that the sons of the establishment in both countries deviate from the prevailing image of members of that stratum as dead-set against loss of wealth through taxation, but also that they are not intensely committed, even at the verbal level, to such a basic reform.

The Costa Ricans affirmed the reform position less than the Panamanians in two cases out of three. This may reflect either a somewhat greater conservatism or the fact that some steps had already been taken to reduce the intensity of "the social problem" there. In any event, the Costa Ricans have experienced partial implementation of the welfare state and their privileged youth appear not to have reacted in opposition to it. The Panamanians have not had a similar experience, and their privileged youth appear not to oppose potential shifts in this direction.

Referring back to the peculiarly strong appeal and critical role of Chiari in Panamanian politics, it is now possible to conclude that his pronouncements in behalf of reform probably struck a responsive chord in most of these students. His reformism was not severely tested however at the time of the first collection of data from this student body. Taking into account both the prevailing reformism of the students and the fact that its intensity diminished concerning one of the most tangible aspects, progressive taxation, it is hard to predict whether support for the President would rise, hold constant, or decline as his administration proved to work no basic policy changes.

NATIONALISM, THE CUBAN REVOLUTION, AND COMMUNISM (TABLE A-6)

Relations with the United States have always been the foremost issue in Panamanian politics. This situation continues, despite the rise of a "social" politics. In fact, the socially radical elements have also been those most sensitive to Panama's dependence on the United States, so that the rise of the new issues has exacerbated the older ones, and these in turn were affected by the messages emanating from

Cuba about the manner in which the Castro government had moved to resolve at the same time the social and the "imperialist" problems. In Costa Rica, virulent nationalism has not occurred, in the sense of a highly intense defensiveness toward the U.S., though there has been concern about the economic relations between the two, inasmuch as the Costa Rican economy is so heavily dependent upon that of the U.S.

The interests of the Panamanian upper class have been well served by the prevailing political system, by the infusion of U.S. dollars directly via the Canal Zone purchases, employment, and other activities, and by the ready, virtually tangible scapegoat Yankee to divert local discontents. Despite this relationship, the Panamanian students, whose fathers have benefited from and substantially shaped this relationship, reflected some of the hostility widely exhibited by their countrymen toward the United States. Responding to the statement, "Essentially Panama (Costa Rica) and the United States are good friends," almost all members of both sets of students agreed, but there were large inter-national differences in the intensity of agreement, with half the Costa Ricans' agreeing strongly compared with less than one-fourth of the Panamanians. This difference carries over to feelings toward North Americans as a whole, as distinct from the previous item's focus on intergovernmental relations. Few Panamanians stated a dislike for North Americans, but only one-third said they like them (the remaining one-half classifying themselves as indifferent). By contrast, two-thirds of the Costa Ricans were positive and almost none were negative. President Kennedy was evaluated negatively by only 1 per cent of either set of students, and positively by everyone else, but where four-fifths of the Costa Ricans strongly approved of him, only half the Panamanians were equally enthusiastic.

Both student groups reacted to U.S. business interests in their countries without intense approval or disapproval, the bulk tending toward non-nationalist positions, but with substantial minorities' disapproving their role. Responding to the proposition that "North American corporations should not be permitted to operate in this country," about three-fifths indicated rejection in some measure of this nationalist position, though only one-fourth did so strongly. With regard to the specific case of the United Fruit Company, a major element in both economies and a leading historical symbol of imperialism, evaluation was surprisingly positive, though again not intensely so. About three-fourths of both groups agreed with the statement, "The United Fruit

Company is beneficial for Panama (Costa Rica)." The overwhelming majority of both sets affirmed that "If the job were good, I would like to work for a North American company in this country," but the Costa Ricans were not only more in agreement but much more intensely so. Thus hostility or reticence toward the United States seems to foreclose for only a minority, even of the Panamanians, the possibility of occupational dependence on U.S. firms.

On the question of the Canal, however, a majority of the Panamanians endorsed nationalist sentiment for ending U.S. control. Over half agreed that "The Panama Canal should be nationalized," although only about half of this number affirmed it strongly. Over half the Costa Ricans joined in support of Panama's "right" to the Canal.

Thus the pattern of nationalist orientations was such that the sons of the elite in Panama exhibited more of the prevailing hostility to or reticence about the United States – government, citizens, business enterprise – than one might have expected on the basis of their fathers' vested interest in prevailing ties to that country, but the intensity of evaluation was moderate, whereas that of other sectors of that society was extreme.[10] A substantial minority of the Costa Ricans appeared to question the role generally of U.S. business in their country, but their feelings about intergovernmental relations and U.S. citizens as a whole were very positive.

The Panamanians did seem, however, to believe considerably more than the Costa Ricans that the international political environment is changing with respect to the distribution of power. Asked whether the United States, the U.S.S.R., the neutrals, or China was likely to be the strongest world power in ten years, less than half of the Panamanians saw the United States in this role, compared with about three-fourths of the Costa Ricans. The fact that the United States was perceived by over half the Panamanians as not dominating future world politics may mean that an important aspect of traditional isthmian power relations may also be perceived as changing. That this has affected the urgency with which local problems and pressures are in turn perceived seems a reasonable hypothesis to account for the relatively reformist position of these students and their overwhelming support for their President.

There seems little division within the ranks of these privileged

[10]Among law students at the national university or students at the major public secondary school, for example, nationalism is much more intense with regard to the range of indicators described above.

students concerning evaluation of the Cuban Revolution and its leadership: it was extremely negative. Almost three-fifths of both groups strongly agreed that "The Cuban Revolution is a bad example for Latin America," and only one-fifth rejected the statement. With virtual unanimity both sets disapproved of Fidel Castro, and most of these felt strongly about it. That this evaluation is closely tied to the position of Cuba within the Communist bloc and the students' opposition to communism is indicated by the fact that virtually all the Panamanians and four-fifths of the Costa Ricans strongly disagreed that "The Communist Party should be legalized in this country." Despite this intense antagonism, the Panamanians particularly seemed plagued where hostility toward the United States conflicted with hostility toward Castro and communism. The Panamanian students were evenly divided on the matter of action to overthrow Castro, half supporting action by the United States or the Organization of American States, and half supporting a policy of inaction or of action only by the Cubans themselves. Only one-fourth of the Costa Ricans took the latter, non-interventionist, position.

It seems clear that Panamanian nationalism has divided the youth of upper-status families in such a manner that a considerable proportion of them side moderately with prevailing opinion. But these Panamanian students appeared, at least as of 1961, to be intensely opposed to those aspects of domestic nationalism that had any affinity for communism or Cuban radicalism. Their position seems very close to that articulated by President Chiari upon his assumption of office in late 1960.

BELIEFS ABOUT MEANS OF POLITICAL CHANGE (TABLE A-7)

One way of estimating beliefs about the limits of changeability in politics is to ask questions about utopia. Asked whether "Social class distinctions are inevitable," three-fifths of each set of students agreed, thereby indicating a conservative view, and less than one-sixth strongly disagreed.

If utopia is not a part of most students' beliefs, what are their beliefs about what is possible through the existing system? If the party system is perceived to involve meaningful competition, then political change may be expected as a possible outcome of the electoral and parliamentary process. There are substantial between-national group differences here, as three-fifths of the Panamanians and two-fifths of the Costa Ricans agreed that "There is not much difference between our political parties." This suggests that more of the Costa Ricans believed that change can emerge via party politics, a belief perhaps predictable from the relatively high proportion of partisan affiliation within that group.

Beyond the limits of the party system, the Panamanians, especially, tended to perceive the freedom of action of officials as severely limited by the prevailing elite, as indicated by their much greater intensity of agreement with the statement, "If any official really tried to resolve basic problems, the rich would prevent it."

Looking at the other limits of change, via social revolution, one finds that over three-fifths of each group believed that "A revolution like the Cuban could not happen in this country," the Panamanians agreeing less intensely, with only a small fraction strongly rejecting the proposition.

Taken together then, the bulk of each group rejected utopian views of the possibility of doing away with the social stratification system, while Costa Ricans were more likely to perceive change resulting from the operation of the party system and more likely to see officials' having freedom of action concerning resolution of basic problems vis-à-vis the stance of the rich. Furthermore, the Costa Ricans affirmed more strongly that social revolution is not likely to be the vehicle of change. The Panamanians tended to see their normal political process as blocking change, so that the reforms they appear to have endorsed seem relatively unlikely to gain implementation under prevailing conditions. This suggests that their apparent faith in the capacity of President Chiari to carry out his stated program is not actually matched by their beliefs concerning the capacity of the present system to accommodate such changes. While these Panamanian students were internally divided on the belief in the likelihood of social revolution, few seemed to believe strongly in such a possibility.

EVALUATION OF MEANS OF POLITICAL CHANGE (TABLE A-8)

Given their positions on policy and their beliefs as to the way in which their political systems work, what were the values held by these students with regard to rules of the political game?

At the outset, democracy as an abstraction seemed highly favored. Responding to the statement, "Democracy is inappropriate for poor nations," over four-fifths of each set rejected it; most of these strongly so. Thus, though the Panamanians in particular saw their system actually likely to block the reforms they favored, they did not appear to reject the general value of constitutional democracy, despite the way in which their variety operates.

An integral part of Western-style constitutional democracy is the freedom to speak and associate for political purposes. Asked about this aspect of democracy (less abstract than the previous item) as follows, "Freedom of speech and assembly should be unlimited," the two groups displayed large differences. Over three-fifths of the Panamanians rejected this civil libertarian position, compared with two-fifths of the Costa Ricans. It is probable that these relatively privileged Panamanian students feared that unlimited political freedom would loose the forces of radicalism, which in a previous section were found to be an object of their strong hostility. It should be emphasized here, however, that a discussion of civil liberties only from the standpoint of the upper-status students is incomplete. It is likely, for example, that untrammeled freedom of speech and assembly in the Panamanian context would lead to the organization of revolutionary political movements uncommitted to these very civil liberties. To indicate this as a probability is not to indicate a normative judgment about the role of civil liberties in transitional societies nor, at least at this point, to indicate a judgment as to the possibility of institutionalizing such rules of the game in these types of societies. In any event, it seems clear that the Costa Ricans' more widespread belief that their political system can accommodate change democratically is matched by their greater commitment to a civil libertarian system that encourages democratic change.

Another way of assessing whether abstract commitments to constitutional democracy are guides to behavior in real political situations is to ask people about the role of violence. About three-fourths of each set of students agreed that "Violence should never be used to settle political problems," with over half taking this position strongly. While this response among the Costa Ricans fits the general pattern of orientation toward their political system, it indicates the ambivalence of the Panamanians on the whole question of the relationship between the good political system and what compromises with it must be made. The bulk of the Panamanians appear to hold that democracy is good even though (as indicated earlier) their actual system falls short of it, but also that democratic liberties cannot be implemented fully, though violence should not be used.

The students were also asked whether "The political parties should be dissolved," and over three-fourths rejected the proposition, the Costa Ricans somewhat more intensely. Again, the Costa Rican pattern fits, but the Panamanian adds to the image of ambivalence in that although most of them saw not much difference between their parties and most seemed dubious about their officials and the prevailing political process, there was an overwhelming shrinking from a proposition that the political system be modified through abolition of the party system.

Finally, the students were confronted with a proposition demanding a choice between effective government and constitutional democratic procedures: "If a government is doing a good job, it should be allowed to remain in power, even though this might mean the postponement of elections." The majority of both sets rejected this thesis, but the Costa Ricans' disagreement was much more intense. Clearly, then, the Panamanians seemed to be closely divided on the general question of commitments to constitutional democracy versus the dangers of its full implementation on the one hand and on the other the need for effective treatment of "the nation's unfinished business."

SUMMARY

The inheritors of the establishment in Panama and Costa Rica are highly sanguine about their future prospects. In Costa Rica an attempt has been made to strike out in a welfare state direction and to incorporate the interests of both middle and lower classes into the political process. Though this has been a halting endeavor, it has been begun and the impact on at least this sample of youth of the establishment has apparently not been basically threatening. Despite the changes, the sons of well-placed families see their future with high optimism. On the other hand, their Panamanian counterparts do not appear to be threatened about their personal future by the rising discontent in their society.

The students' perceptions of general opportunity for mobility in their societies are notable for their near congruence, though differences do exist in a direction predictable from widespread images of the two societies. It is from this point on, however, that the patterns of orientation diverge. The Costa Ricans tend to see the limitations on opportunity that exist, but they see their political system as an open one, which suggests that the problems can be treated politically, at least in their view, within the system. (This may have personal relevance for them as well, inasmuch as a substantial majority of them see the need for considerable change if they are to attain the influence they want. Believing this, they apparently are not frustrated or alienated, because the system is perceived as manipulable.) A very large percentage of them are affiliated psychologically with a party, and, given the nature of the party system, this is an integrative element. The predominant party affiliation is with the PLN, the majority welfare statist party, the organization and style of which are the most modern of the three major parties. Thus, the party that most threatened the old order has been able to recruit a substantial proportion of the sons of the establishment. And finally, despite the intensity of the PLN supporters within this group, the other parties are evaluated with less than intense disapproval, an indicator of accommodative orientations on the part of these students.

The Costa Rican students tend to be critical about the corruptibility of their politicians, and yet at the same time, the great bulk of them think that the public officials work in the public interest. The incumbent (PLN) President was overwhelmingly approved, as was his (PUN-PRN) predecessor. The system, then, seems to be highly legitimate in the eyes of this student group.

Perhaps because of their conservatism, or perhaps because a beginning has been made toward the amelioration of some of the pressing social problems, the Costa Rican students are not intensely reformist; however, a substantial majority agree that problems exist in the agrarian and tax collection areas, and that full employment policies are desirable. Taken together with the data on personal expectations and predominant PLN affiliation, this is substantial evidence that the changes in the system since 1948 have been accepted by the sons of the establishment.

In comparison with their Panamanian counterparts, the Costa Ricans believe that their party system affords meaningful competition, and they overwhelmingly reject the proposition that prolongation of an effective government might justify manipulation of the electoral process. They strongly endorse democracy in the abstract as appropriate even for poor countries, and concerning the more specific aspect of constitutional democracy—freedom of speech and assembly—they also tend to take the civil libertarian position. Thus, although many of them see the rich as exercising substantial constraints on the officials as the latter confront national problems, the generally consistent pattern of orientations indicates their perception of the system as open, flexible, and meaningfully accommodative of national problems.

Given the fact that the United States plays a very prominent role in the country, and that potentially at least the Alliance for Progress provides an important opportunity for assaulting some outstanding national problems, it is significant that these establishment youths of Costa Rica view the U.S. in its public and private corporate aspects not uncritically (there is obvious concern about the role of U.S. corporations locally) but with overwhelming friendliness. This means that, insofar as these students are concerned, the Alliance faces fewer of the problems of establishing a dialogue or of erasing traditional hostilities than it does elsewhere in Latin America, including Panama.

The Panamanians' pattern of orientation is much more mixed. Their evaluation of the political system includes positive, ambivalent, and negative elements, with disapproval characterizing their view of politicians and officials. Only half of them are integrated into the party system. The only element evoking enthusiasm is the President, of whom there is virtually total approval. Given the President's position on reform and the fact that the great majority of these students endorse reform, though not intensely, it seems reasonable to conclude that one factor accounting for the absence of general support for the system is its rigidity in the face of demands for social change. In contrast with the Costa Ricans, these students perceive their system as closed and rigid in this regard. The parties are viewed as not providing alternatives, and the rich are perceived as constraining any official who might seek seriously to attack outstanding problems. The students are fairly evenly divided (the narrow majority opposed) over the desirability of effective government if this were to require delay of elections. Yet the students overwhelmingly oppose the dissolution of the existing parties and reject the use of force as an answer to political problems. Similarly, virtually all of them reject Communist or *fidelista* approaches. Thus in many ways they seem to mirror the President, in that his moderate reformism coexists with a disposition not to attempt major political changes, even though the existing system operates to block the proposed reforms and lacks any mechanism whereby power might be mobilized in their behalf. These orientations taken together make it difficult to predict the students' reaction to Chiari's inability over time to make headway on his program. It is conceivable, in view both of his great popularity among them and of the presumed disposition of many Latin American intellectuals to express reformism but not to act on it, that his mere expression of a progressive program would be sufficient to insure his continued support among the sons of the establishment, for some regardless of, for others because of, his inability to implement that program.

This group of Panamanians cannot be characterized as strongly hostile to the United States, but their marked reserve toward U.S. government, U.S. control of the Canal, and the role of U.S. corporations means that the Alliance is unlikely to mobilize their enthusiastic support. This is important because they appear to represent the greatest potential support for the Alliance, given the extreme nationalism of other, socially less privileged elements of the population, particularly the younger intellectuals. On the other hand, the quality of attitudes indicates that these upper-status students are unlikely to support a radical nationalist movement either, so that, as with their other political orientations, the prevailing pattern may be one of ambivalence and perhaps immobilism. These possibilities can be better assessed with the introduction of data from a later point in time.

CHAPTER V

CHANGING ORIENTATIONS: THE PANAMANIANS AT TIME 2

APPROXIMATELY TWENTY-SIX MONTHS AFTER THE FIRST COLLECTION of data on political orientations from the Panamanian students, another questionnaire was given to a similar set of students in the same school, though the individuals were different. This chapter assesses and analyzes the extent and direction of changes in orientations, and again compares Panamanian students at Time 2 with Costa Ricans.

A brief summary of changes and continuities over this time period in Panamanian politics will be given. (These were developed at greater length in Chapter III.)

The circumstances of President Chiari's orderly election in May, 1960, and assumption of office in October, 1960, were relatively unprecedented. He was an opposition candidate in the election, and yet neither the typical claims of electoral manipulation nor post-election threats to deny him office occurred. Coming to office at perhaps the height of Castro's hemispheric popularity and at a time when democratic alternatives to the Cuban model were being examined by Latin intellectuals ever more critically, he publicly alerted the country to what he considered to be an emerging crisis of underdevelopment and rising expectation. He clearly and publicly identified himself as a member of the old ruling family clique and suggested that either the latter would make concerted efforts to meet the crisis through social and economic reforms or the consequence would be loss of leadership to those committed to extreme changes. He constrained local *fidelista* and other radical political activity, backed the U.S. position on Castro, and sought both extensive Alliance for Progress commitments and cooperation with the United States in meeting Panamanian demands concerning the Canal treaty.

During this time, the economy was expanding, ending a protracted period of postwar stagnation, although the pattern of distribution of wealth probably did not change concomitantly.

The moderate, reformist, constitutionalist stance of Chiari seemed to be congruent generally with the political orientations of this group of well-off students. On the other hand, the nature of the ambivalence detected in the students' responses at Time 1 coincided with the most difficult obstacles the President faced in carrying out his program. For example, the students lacked faith in the party system, and only a relatively small proportion felt any affiliation with a party. In the face of a legislature dominated by the oligarchy, mobilization of public support for new and threatening policies would depend on the organization of a new and policy-oriented party (or the reorganization in this manner of an old one). This seemed a particularly important task because the Panamanian Presidential term of office is a short four years, and the experience with regard to past attempts at reform indicated little continuity across administrations. Furthermore, Chiari himself lacked the charismatic quality that might have served to mobilize the public in the absence of or as a first stage in the development of a mass-based political organization.

Thus, over this two-year period, leadership had been exercised so as to raise the expectations of the discontented for reform and development. This leadership had identified itself publicly as an experiment in an oligarchically controlled constitutional democracy's capacity to accomplish tasks of this order, and the experiment was also publicly identified as dependent substantially on an Alliance directed by what was widely considered to be an imperially superordinate government, and this at a time of ascendant nationalism locally and worldwide.

The structure of power and the rules of the political game remained essentially constant over this period of time, however. The "experiment" under Chiari did not result in basic policy changes generally, and the few reform laws that were passed were not implemented in such a way as to constitute major changes. Furthermore, aside from structural continuity, there was no indication of a change in orientation under way within the oligarchy, no signs of an internal debate or even of some unthinkable thoughts. By the time of the second survey of students' orientations, the 1964 Presidential election campaign was in its first stages, on a traditional basis and with a traditional cast.

This, then, provides a setting for the reassessment of political orientations of the sons of the establishment. Whether or not the inchoate but developing demands for change by the discontented and the expressions from the Presidency of the need for change and the lack of action on the latter proposals contributed to substantial changes in the students' orientations will now be estimated.

EXPECTATIONS ABOUT PERSONAL SUCCESS (TABLE A-1)[1]

The high level of confidence about their future success continued to characterize the students at Time 2. A substantial shift occurred with regard to only one of the six items used to assess this orientational dimension, and that shift was across a narrow range, essentially from disagreement to slight (as opposed to "some" or "strong") agreement that "Only if things change very much will I attain the success I want." Apparently expectations for personal success were generally unaffected by political dynamics in Panama over the two-year period. The sons of the establishment in Panama and Costa Rica continued to exhibit quite similar high expectations.

BELIEFS ABOUT OTHERS' CHANCES FOR SUCCESS (TABLE A-2)

The moderate to strong inter-national differences in belief about others' chances for success increased by Time 2. One response to national political events appears to have been more recognition of the rigidity of class lines on the part of the Panamanian students. Moderate shifts (10–16 per cent) occurred in a consistent pattern increasing the differences noted at Time 1, so that the Panamanians at Time 2 contrasted sharply with the Costa Ricans concerning the belief that "One can succeed in this country with ability and effort," "The majority of the good things in life are controlled by the few," and "There is no racial discrimination in this country." The moderate and strong differences on two further items remained constant.

POLITICIZATION (TABLE A-3)

Inconsistent shifts occurred in this area. Political participation appeared to decrease slightly from Time 1 to Time 2 among the

[1]The tables for this chapter are also found in Appendix A, pp. 103-13.

Panamanians. An exception to this pattern was the extremely sharp decline in frequent discussion of the Cuban Revolution (from 62 to 37 per cent). At the same time, a slight to moderate rise in politicization was reported on every one of the items concerning psychological involvement in politics. These patterns suggest that the response to the political stagnation following Chiari's pronouncement of a reform program was not the initiation or heightening of a debate among the sons of the establishment on the politics of social justice, but the intensification of their interest in politics caused by the problems this kind of new politics raised for them. For example, political discussion and participation in student demonstrations declined slightly over time, but a larger proportion of the students also rejected the proposition that "What the government does will not affect my life very much." Furthermore, the incidence of content sensitivity in response to the questionnaire rose markedly among the Panamanians from Time 1 to Time 2, a shift that was largely a function of the increased salience of the subscale based on evaluation of politicians.[2]

EVALUATION OF THE POLITICAL SYSTEM (TABLE A-4)

By Time 2, President Chiari had lost his strongest support among the students and had become the object of disapproval for a sizable minority. Where 38 per cent had strongly approved of the President two years earlier, 10 per cent did so at Time 2, while approval in some measure dropped from 87 to 53 per cent, and disapproval rose from a mere 4 per cent to 32 per cent. (That this does not merely reflect the "normal" loss of popularity of any administration as it develops a record is indicated by the substantial decline in support for the President preceding Chiari as well.) A concomitant decline occurred with regard to the evaluation of the Chiari government as a whole. The proportion agreeing that "The government is doing a good job in resolving basic problems" dropped from 83 per cent in 1961 to 47 per cent in 1963. With reference to the specific policy area of housing ("The government is doing all in its power to provide adequate housing for the poor"), total agreement declined from 88 to 53 per cent, and strong agreement from 45 to 13 per cent, indicating the disappointment of extremely high hopes for amelioration of Panama's severe tenement and shack-town problems.

---

[2]Content sensitivity—response to item substance rather than item format—is defined, measured, and assessed for theoretical purposes in Appendix C.

The decline in Chiari's standing with the students, apparently as a result of his failure to implement a program of reform and development, had a critical impact on the students' accordance of legitimacy to the political system. As was indicated earlier, Chiari's popularity and the expectations raised by his first declarations had been the one strongly positive factor in the students' evaluations of the system at Time 1. From that point to Time 2, there had been a substantial weakening in support for the system or ambivalence about it. For example, with regard to the query whether "Politics and government are helpful to the country, harmful, or neither," the proportion of positive responses fell from 54 to 27 per cent (compared with 54 per cent of the Costa Ricans), while the negatives rose from 19 to 37 per cent (compared with 11 per cent of the Costa Ricans). The proportion evaluating politics and government as "honest" fell from 22 to 8 per cent (compared with 24 per cent of the Costa Ricans), while the proportion responding "dishonest" rose from 22 to 44 per cent (compared with 8 per cent of the Costa Ricans).

The incapacity of the existing political parties to integrate even these well-off students in this situation is indicated by the slight decline in the proportion perceiving themselves affiliated with any party from 53 to 44, in contrast with 79 per cent of the Costa Ricans.

Substantial inter-national differences existed at Time 1 with regard to evaluation of public officials as a group. By Time 2 the percentage of students disagreeing with the proposition that "The majority of the public officials work in behalf of the public welfare" had risen from 64 to 81 (compared with 38 per cent of the Costa Ricans), with a rise in strong disagreement from 26 to 42 per cent (compared with 11 per cent of the Costa Ricans). The very large international differences in response to the proposition that "A great many politicians sell themselves easily" increased slightly from Time 1 to Time 2.

In addition to the aforementioned comparisons of evaluation at different points in time, two indicators used in the Costa Rican questionnaire were included in the second Panamanian questionnaire. One of these presented an extreme proposition about politicians as a whole: "All our politicians are worth nothing." The other provided an over-all evaluation of the system: "Our system of government and politics is good for the country." The profundity of these Panamanian students' rejection of present political arrangements at Time 2 was indicated in their responses: 62 per cent endorsed the extreme statement about their politicians, compared with 32 per cent of the Costa Ricans. Only 4 per cent of the Panamanians agreed strongly that the system was good for the country, compared with 36 per cent of the Costa Ricans; only 22 per cent of the Panamanians agreed somewhat, compared with 72 per cent of the Costa Ricans, and the total proportion of all degrees of agreement on this basic proposition was 40 in Panama and 92 in Costa Rica.

Clearly the patterns of response at the two points in time indicate that a major shift had occurred in the pattern of evaluations of the political system. As of Time 2, a substantial majority of those most likely to support the existing system, the sons of the establishment, had shifted from prevailing ambivalence to a much more oppositionalist stance. Not only were officials and politicians as a group largely opposed by the students, but the system as a whole was rejected by a majority, and virtually none strongly supported it. It would appear possible that at least indirectly the process of demoralization of the incumbent elite had begun. We have no data on the evaluations of that incumbent elite itself, but if its members were unable to win the allegiance of their own sons to the existing system, then the moral position of that elite would appear to have begun to disintegrate.

POSITIONS ON SOME REFORM ISSUES (TABLE A-5)

Substantial shifts in orientation toward reform occurred over time, increasing the differences between the Panamanian and Costa Rican students. For example, 25 per cent of the latter agreed strongly on the need for agrarian reform compared with 41 per cent of the Panamanians at Time 1; by Time 2, 53 per cent of the Panamanians endorsed this need strongly. Panamanian reformism had appeared as hesitant as the Costa Rican at Time 1 in relation to the specific proposition that "The rich should pay much higher taxes than they do now." At Time 2, however, extreme support for this position had grown from 25 to 38 per cent among the Panamanians, compared with 19 per cent among the Costa Ricans, and the proportion agreeing at least somewhat had grown from 37 to 54 per cent, compared with 32 per cent among the Costa Ricans. An additional datum available at Time 2 showed that 61 per cent of the Panamanians thought that "The rich should yield their privileges," compared with but 36 per cent of the Costa Ricans.

The pattern conforms with the hypothesis that Chiari's standing among these students at Time 1 was substantially a function of his expressed reformism, and that his ineffectiveness in this regard was the major factor both in his loss of support and in the shift in legitimacy orientations. The rise in reformism and decline in legitimacy also indicate that the current of discontent to which Chiari originally responded and to which he gave impetus was a substantial one, and not merely a manifestation of Latin Americans' seeking gratification through expressive behavior without concern for implementation.

NATIONALISM, THE CUBAN REVOLUTION, AND COMMUNISM (TABLE A-6)

Inasmuch as Chiari's original program was so heavily dependent on the Alliance for Progress and on the resolution of outstanding U.S.-Panamanian differences over the Canal, and since the U.S. had proceeded to develop a large-scale Alliance program in Panama, the domestic failure to organize a political movement capable of sustaining a reform program left the U.S. effort impossible of fulfillment. In such circumstances it would not be surprising if the consequence were heightened nationalism as frustrations were vented against the dominant external "enemy." As a matter of fact, nationalism appeared to be calmed during the early years of the Chiari administration, as Alliance efforts mounted and as Panama and the United States began protracted talks on the Canal treaty. Then in January, 1964, the riots showed how superficial this "calm" had been and how broad and deep the nationalist current had become.

At Time 2 (just about three months before the riots), the sons of the establishment appeared strongly divided in their orientation toward the United States, with changes apparent both in a negative and in a positive direction. Though Kennedy remained very popular among the Panamanian students, there was considerable diminution in their approval of him. In response to the contention that "Essentially the United States and this country are good friends," there was a decline in strong agreement from 23 per cent at Time 1 to 13 per cent at Time 2 (compared with 51 per cent among the Costa Ricans), while the proportion agreeing at least somewhat fell from 62 to 40 per cent (compared with 93 per cent among the Costa Ricans).

On the other hand, these students appeared to have lost some confidence in the desirability or capacity of political and economic nationalism to contribute to an improvement in the condition of the country. On the overridingly important issue of the Canal, they seemed to be moving away from the mainstream of opinion. The proportion disagreeing that "The Canal should be nationalized" rose from 44 to 54 per cent. These students, in sharp contrast to their counterparts in public high schools (such as the Instituto Nacional, whence the originators of the January riots issued) and the University, seemed as time passed to be losing confidence in the country's capacity for assertive, independent action. Where 60 per cent disagreed at Time 1 that "The Panamanians can operate the Canal without help from the North Americans," 72 per cent did so at Time 2. Furthermore, a slightly larger majority at Time 2 disagreed that "North American corporations should not be permitted to operate in this country." If radical nationalism was increasing in Panama, and it was based on the belief that great and sweeping changes could be made in the country's institutions, as has been recently the case in Cuba, Egypt, Algeria, China, etc., then the sons of the establishment despite their growing reformism may have moved farther away from the center of change in the two years covered by the present study.

Their position did not appear to have changed very much concerning Castro or communism. At Time 2 a larger minority than at Time 1 disagreed that "The Cuban Revolution is a bad example for Latin America," but a change in the same degree occurred in the other direction concerning the desirability of action to overthrow Castro. The legalization of the Communist party continued to be opposed by over 80 per cent of the students, as was the case with the Costa Ricans. So far, then, the illegitimacy of the political system had not become associated with heightened nationalism or a more accommodating position vis-à-vis the Cuban approach to reform and development. What, then, were the students' perceptions of likely means to political change?

BELIEFS ABOUT MEANS OF POLITICAL CHANGE (TABLE A-7)

Panamanian students became even less utopian over time in regard to the inevitability of class distinctions. At the same time, however, they appeared to become more convinced that change was improbable under prevailing conditions. The percentage who believed "There is not much difference between our political parties" rose from 59 to 71, in contrast with but 37 per cent of the Costa Ricans. There was a similar shift concerning the perception that the rich would not tolerate basic changes. In response to the statement that "If any official really tried to resolve basic problems, the rich would prevent it," the percentage of strong agreement rose slightly from 29 to 37, compared with 11 per cent of the Costa Ricans, and over-all agreement rose from 61 to 73, compared with 50 per cent of the latter.

There was also a lessening interest in the country's only reform movement as a means to change. Christian Democracy has been a diffuse, little-developed movement in Panama and has appeared to have a great deal of support among moderate elements of the establishment. It included these students as enthusiastic adherents at Time 1. But at Time 2, although it continued to find widespread favor among them, its failure to materialize as a tangible political alternative was reflected in the decline of those strongly disagreeing that "Christian Democracy will be incapable of making the changes the country needs" from 58 to 37 per cent.

Another set of items that were used in the Costa Rican study and only the Time 2 part of the Panamanian study provides data in the same pattern. About half of both Costa Ricans and Panamanians believed the rich could be persuaded to yield their privileges (though the issue was perceived as much less problematic and intense among the Costa Rican students), but 34 per cent of the Panamanians in contrast with 21 per cent of the Costa Ricans thought that "Force will be necessary to make the rich yield their privileges." Lack of faith in the legislative process among the Panamanians at Time 2 is indicated by the fact that only 33 per cent of them agreed strongly that "The legislative assembly is very important in this country," compared with 61 per cent of the Costa Ricans.

The students were asked how much they believed each of the following means would improve their economic situation: the Alliance for Progress, social reform, social revolution, and the maintenance of present institutions. (Each was presented separately for evaluation with regard to its likelihood of improving one's situation much, some, or not at all. The following analysis focuses only on the "much" response alternative.) The major difference lies in the Costa Ricans' much greater belief in the Alliance's making much improvement – 68 per cent of them responded this way compared with 31 per cent of the Panamanians. "Social reform" was cited in this fashion twice as much by the Panamanians as were "social revolution" or "maintenance of present institutions" (43 per cent to 22 per cent and 21 per cent), showing still the tendency of a large minority toward moderation. Yet it should be noted that a much larger minority of the Panamanians than of the Costa Ricans (22 to 4 per cent) believed strongly in the efficacy of the extreme, "social revolution" approach.

As change became perceived as less likely through the prevailing system, the belief in the likelihood of revolutionary change rose dramatically. Sixty-nine per cent of the Costa Ricans and 62 per cent of the Panamanians agreed at Time 1 that "A revolution like the Cuban cannot happen in this country," but by Time 2, the percentage of Panamanians in agreement had dropped to 35. This raises the further question whether preferences concerning more extreme measures in politics changed correspondingly.

EVALUATION OF MEANS OF POLITICAL CHANGE (TABLE A-8)

The pattern of evaluations of political means is one of a shift away from constitutional democracy in favor of more *effective* means of bringing about major changes, but the pattern involves some major inconsistencies or incongruities.

At Time 1, slightly more of the Panamanians than Costa Ricans (68 to 61 per cent) strongly rejected the proposition that "Democracy is inappropriate for poor countries," but by Time 2 the percentage of strong disagreement had fallen to 49. There was a slight decline over time in opposition to unlimited freedom of speech and assembly. Taken in context with other responses, this probably reflects rising dissatisfaction with the prevailing rules of the game more than it does growing support for civil liberties per se. Devaluation of the party system is evident in the marked drop in percentage of those opposed to dissolving the parties—strong disagreement with this proposition declined over time from 40 to 27 per cent, compared with 53 per cent of the Costa Ricans; at least substantial disagreement fell from 60 to 43 per cent, compared with 74 per cent of the Costa Ricans. It was noted in the previous section that belief in the efficacy of Christian Democracy had declined. Strong agreement that it provides "the formula for resolving national problems" also fell correspondingly from 59 to 37 per cent over time.

The increasing preference for *effective* government is reflected in the lessened opposition to the proposition that, "If a government is doing a good job, it should remain in office, even if this means postponing elections." At Time 1, 55 per cent of the Panamanians disagreed with this, compared with 71 per cent of the Costa Ricans, but by Time 2 the percentage had dropped to 42.

Very large inter-national differences appear in response to another item showing disenchantment with constitutional government: "More than legislation, more than politicians, what this country needs is a leader in whom the people can place their confidence." The incidence of strong agreement for the Panamanians at Time 2 (the item was not included at Time 1) and for the Costa Ricans, respectively, was 46 and 25 per cent, and the total percentage of agreement, 73 and 46.

The Panamanians also were less supportive of either prevailing political economic arrangements or moderate alternatives. The students were asked which of the following was the best solution for national problems: capitalism, Marxism, indigenous socialism, and the various combinations of the three. Responses including capitalism or indigenous socialism or a combination of the two were given by 75 per cent of the Costa Ricans but by only 40 per cent of the Panamanians at Time 2 (the item was not included earlier). Significantly, the difference tends to be more a negative one than one of the Panamanians' opting for the more extreme alternatives. That is, their responses were diffused among the other alternatives, a range of written-in alternatives, and no answer at all.

Despite the disenchantment with the prevailing order, however, the Panamanians appeared extremely opposed to the use of force to accomplish political change. For example, there was no change over time in their level of agreement that "Violence should never be used to decide political questions." Half of them, and of the Costa Ricans, continued strongly to agree to this, and three-fourths agreed in some measure. And, on a basic preference concerning the risks of change—"Social change is acceptable only when it does not provoke disorder"—there were only 18 per cent of the Panamanian students at Time 2 who disagreed, the same percentage as among the Costa Ricans, who faced much less pressure for that kind of change.

SUMMARY AND CONCLUSIONS

Over time, the patterns of political orientations of the sons of the establishment in Panama and Costa Rica have become much more distinct. In contrast with the Panamanians, the Costa Rican students feel much more positive about their political system and are much more integrated into it through the party system (which has served to integrate other classes as well). They see much greater opportunity for mobility in society and polity. Though they see the need for reform in difficult areas, they seem much more to believe that such problems can be accommodated through the existing system.

The sons of the establishment in Panama seem overwhelmingly to think that the prevailing structure of power and rules of the game are inappropriate. The system has lost most of its legitimate aspects, and ambivalence has substantially shifted toward opposition. This pattern of legitimacy orientations seems largely a function of the students' belief in the need for sweeping reforms and economic development policies. They have come increasingly to perceive the social and political system as static, as severely limiting social and political mobility, and unlike other privileged Latin American groups, they appear to have evaluated such a system as bad for the country. Quite conceivably, this shift toward oppositionalism would not have occurred if Chiari had not behaved in extraordinary fashion by expressing so continuously and vehemently the need for profound reform. This may have generated at least among the sons of the establishment the belief that the country was in trouble. Accepting this redefinition of the situation, and expecting ameliorating action, they observed little change over time, and became disillusioned. Furthermore, they have lost faith, apparently as a result of the Chiari "experiment," in the capacity of the system to change through normal means, that is, through the operation of the version of constitutional democracy that has developed in Panama. As the perception of the system as closed and resistant to gradual change has grown, so has the belief in the likelihood of extreme, revolutionary change. In this, too, the Panamanian sons of the establishment appear more attuned to the winds of change than other similarly situated Latin American groups. Their observation of the obstacles to change has led to an increasing recognition of and preference for effective government and strong leadership, even at the expense of unconstitutional action. But this is as far, apparently, as the great majority are willing to go with political experimentation. Violence is overwhelmingly abhorred, and only a small minority prefers social change if it also means social disorder.

This pattern of orientations may well describe a syndrome of immobilism, if the disinclination to the use of force and the fear of disorder lead to inaction by the students or constrain them from participating in discussions and attempts to organize the partisans of change. But if these students may be constrained from such politically innovative behavior, they may also be constrained from vigorously opposing the revolutionary activity of others, and this could have important consequences for the success of a movement from below committed to political change.

The possibility of immobilism is also suggested (but certainly not demonstrated) by the data on shifts in politicization over time. As the political system becomes more brittle, as the students become extremely disillusioned and cynical about it, as they increasingly perceive the extreme unlikelihood of transforming the system through ordinary means, and as they look in vain for a political channel through which to give vent to these views, overt political participation declines. Given the scope of the problems they see and the virtual absence of creative thinking about them going on in establishment circles, and the suspicion directed against potential "traitors to our class," plus the fact of their virtual isolation from the centers of dissident thought in the public secondary schools, the slight decline in discussion generally and the precipitous drop in discussion of the Cuban Revolution become more comprehensible. It is not easy to be politically active and conversant under these circumstances. What perhaps attests to the seriousness of the students' concern for change is that they have not reacted—as have many other historical counterparts—by complete withdrawal from the world of politics. To the contrary, they appear to have become even more psychologically involved in it, to have become even more aware of the direct relevance of government and politics to their lives. But they may be unwilling to initiate action in the direction they have come to conclude is necessary, because of the extreme risks to established elements involved in processes of rapid change.

If fear of disorder and violence invokes hesitancy about change on the part of these students, their orientation toward nationalism may divert them from the mainstream of change. They lack faith in the Alliance, and the intensity of their psychological ties to the United States—low at Time 1 compared with the Costa Ricans'—has diminished. But they face the uncertainties of the future with less faith over time in the nation's capacity for independent development; their disposition to nationalize the Canal and their confidence in the national capacity to operate it have declined, and they are less oriented toward limitation of the involvement of North American capital in the economy. The greatest changes in transitional societies, however, have come through mobilization of the society by nationalist movements. These are assertive movements, whose leaders generate mass support by dramatizing the situation and potential of the nation.[3] Through the mobilization of mass support the leaders have developed the power resource to sustain them in their reformation of the society. One of the major ways of dramatizing the capacity of the nation to mold its environment has been to nationalize a large and complex industry or facility traditionally in foreign hands and to proceed to operate it with domestic resources. Thus nationalization of the oil industry functioned in Cárdenas' Mexico of 1938, thus did Nasser nationalize the Suez Canal, and Castro a range of utilities and industries in Cuba. The trend in Panamanian politics has been that, while social reform has languished, nationalism has grown in the direction of becoming an assertive movement. Far more than any movement for social reform, nationalism has mobilized the Panamanian populace, and the demand has arisen and gathered force that the Yankees be driven from the isthmus. Regardless of whether or not this approach to national development is good or necessary, if this is the tendency of national politics, the lack of national self-confidence of the sons of the establishment will tend to isolate them.

In summary, then, it seems to me that the sons of the establishment in Panama are likely to make their major contribution to political change by demoralizing the incumbent elite, rather than by active involvement in a movement committed to change, particularly insofar as the latter may have the characteristics of radical nationalism. If their shifting pattern of orientations describes a trend toward "desertion of the intellectuals" in Panama, it is, so far, a desertion from the existing order but not a desertion to another.

---

[3]On the development of this thesis, see Gideon Sjoberg, "Political Structure, Ideology, and Economic Development," a paper prepared for the Carnegie Seminar on Political and Administrative Development, Department of Government, Indiana University, 1963.

CHAPTER VI

CORRELATES OF LEGITIMACY ORIENTATIONS

THE DECLINE IN LEGITIMACY OF THE PANAMANIAN POLITICAL system and the relatively high level of support for the Costa Rican accorded by the sons of the establishment have been generally described. This chapter is concerned with the extent to which legitimacy orientations form policy and ideological syndromes. That is, support, acquiescence, and opposition may logically vary in their degree of association with one or another policy alternative and one or another ideology. Panamanian oppositionalism, for example, could be crystallized in a coherent direction, involving extraordinary expansion of the scope of government in economic, social, and political matters to such a degree that a totalitarian model of mobilization and development is embraced; or it could be diffuse and utterly lacking in direction; or it could combine elements in such a way that immobilism rather than purposeful action would seem likely to ensue. Hypothetically, the apparently very small degree of opposition among the sons of the Costa Rican elite to their system may be more potent than size would indicate as a function of their extremely coherent reactionary orientations, which find an outlet in hyperactive restorationist organizations. In the following, then, an assessment will be made of the coherence of legitimacy orientations, with a view to somewhat more precise projections of their consequences for national politics in the future.

THE LEGITIMACY INDEX

The relevant components of the political system, as stated earlier, are conceived for Latin American politics to be the rules of the game or regime and the power structure. Political community is not a matter

Figure VI-1. FORMATION OF THE LEGITIMACY INDEX

		"The majority of the public officials work in behalf of the public welfare."	
		Agree	Disagree
"In general our system of government and politics is good for the country."	Agree	Support	Ambivalent
	Disagree	Ambivalent	Opposition

of contention;[1] these citizens are not divided over the desirability of membership in their national political community.

An index based on evaluations of these two components was formed by combining responses to the following items:

> In general, our system of politics and government is good for the country.
>
> The majority of the public officials work in behalf of the public welfare.

The first item, although general, was designed to elicit evaluation of the manner in which the political process operates, while the second was focused directly on evaluation of an important category of decision-makers, the officials.

Both items had the same response format: a set of six alternatives ranging from three degrees of agreement through three degrees of disagreement. Because of the relatively small samples involved in this study, the responses were dichotomized simply by agreement-disagreement for the purpose of index construction. Agreement with both statements was taken to indicate a positive evaluation of the political system, disagreement with both as a negative evaluation, and a combination of agreement and disagreement as an ambivalent evaluation.

Because of this dichotomy, it was not possible here to distinguish the Neutrals—those who responded in the least polarized manner—opting a combination of slight agreement and slight disagreement. Given the six-point scale items, such respondents would be the closest approximations of the Neutral acquiescent type, by least supporting *and* least opposing the system. The present intermediate category,

[1]This is not to say that political community lacks importance in regard to Latin American politics. The nature of the political system is affected substantially by the extent to which the citizens have a self-conscious image as citizens of a nation. K. H. Silvert's work on nationalism has been extremely useful in this regard. See his theoretical introduction to *Expectant Peoples* (New York: Random House, 1963).

Table VI-1. Responses to the Two Legitimacy Items

	Panamanians %	Costa Ricans %
"In general our system of government and politics is good for the country."		
Strong Agreement	4	36
Some Agreement	18	36
Slight Agreement	18	19
Slight Disagreement	16	3
Some Disagreement	22	3
Strong Disagreement	20	1
Not Ascertained	2	1
Total %	100	99
N	(90)	(72)
"The majority of the public officials work in behalf of the public welfare"		
Strong Agreement	1	14
Some Agreement	1	21
Slight Agreement	14	26
Slight Disagreement	17	10
Some Disagreement	22	17
Strong Disagreement	42	11
Not Ascertained	2	1
Total %	99	100
N	(90)	(72)

Ambivalence – a combination of one positive and one negative response – may also, however, be treated as probably an acquiescent type, if the positive and negative elements are considered likely to neutralize each other so as to preclude the accordance either of support or opposition to the system. (In any event, as will be shown below, these considerations are tangential to this study because the distributions for Panamanians and Costa Ricans were actually so different that different cutting points between types of orientations were used. That is, the distributions were such that we can deal only with distinctions between primarily ambivalent versus oppositionalist Panamanians, and supportive versus primarily ambivalent Costa Ricans.)

The distribution of responses to the two legitimacy items and the index distributions followed the same pattern essentially. Not only was the proportion of positive evaluations much higher among the

Table VI-2. CROSS-TABULATION OF RESPONSES TO THE TWO LEGITIMACY ITEMS, BY PER CENT

PANAMANIANS

		"... officials work for public welfare."					
		1	2	3	4	5	6
	1	–	–	–	–	–	4.7
	2	–	1.2	3.5	5.8	5.8	2.3
"... system good	3	1.2	–	7.0	4.7	3.5	1.2
for the country."	4	–	–	–	5.8	7.0	3.5
	5	–	–	3.5	–	4.7	14.0
	6	–	–	–	1.2	2.3	17.4

COSTA RICANS

		"... officials work for public welfare."					
		1	2	3	4	5	6
	1	11.3	8.5	9.9	1.4	4.2	1.4
	2	1.4	12.7	12.7	4.2	4.2	1.4
"... system good	3	1.4	–	2.8	2.8	5.6	7.0
for the country."	4	–	–	1.4	1.4	–	–
	5	–	–	–	–	2.8	–
	6	–	–	–	–	1.4	–

Key: 1 – Strong Agreement
2 – Some Agreement
3 – Slight Agreement
4 – Slight Disagreement
5 – Some Disagreement
6 – Strong Disagreement

Costa Ricans than among the Panamanians, but the Costa Ricans tended toward a strongly positive position while the Panamanians tended toward the strongly negative pole. Agreement that "... the system ... is good for the country" was given by 92 per cent of the Costa Ricans and only 40 per cent of the Panamanians; furthermore, 36 per cent of the former were strongly agreed compared with 4 per cent of the latter, and 72 per cent of the former were at least substantially agreed compared with 22 per cent of the latter; while 42 per cent of the Panamanians were at least in substantial disagreement compared with only 4 per cent of the Costa Ricans. Although Costa Ricans are less sanguine about their public officials than about operation of the system in general, they contrasted sharply with the Panamanians here as well, with 61 per cent making a positive evaluation, compared with 17 per cent of the latter. Only 2 per cent of the

Table VI-3. CLASSIFICATION OF STUDENTS BY LEGITIMACY ORIENTATION TYPE, BY PER CENT

	Panamanians %	Costa Ricans %
Supporters		
Agreement on both items	13	60
Ambivalents		
Agreement on one item		
Disagreement on other	31	34
Opponents		
Disagreement on both items	56	6
Total %	100	100
N	(86)	(71)

Panamanians agreed at least substantially that the "... officials work for the public welfare" compared with 35 per cent of the Costa Ricans.

Classification of the students by the index of legitimacy orientations reveals the proportion *supporting* the system as 60 per cent of the Costa Ricans and 13 per cent of the Panamanians, the proportion *ambivalent* about the system as 34 per cent of the Costa Ricans and 31 per cent of the Panamanians, and the proportion *opposing* the system as 6 per cent of the Costa Ricans and 56 per cent of the Panamanians.

Given the size of the samples, it is readily apparent that this pair of distributions precludes a comparison of the policy and ideological correlates of support, ambivalence, and opposition among Panamanians and Costa Ricans. The 6 per cent of the Costa Ricans who opposed the system and the 13 per cent of the Panamanians who supported it are too small for such an analysis. The problem is reinforced by the fact that the form of the two distributions is, in effect, reversed, so that comparative analysis of supporters and of opponents in the two countries is foreclosed. What can be done, however, is to analyze comparatively those who tend toward support and those who tend toward opposition, keeping in mind that (1) the former group in Panama is composed primarily of ambivalents while its Costa Rican counterpart is composed wholly of supporters, and (2) the latter group in Panama is composed wholly of opponents while its Costa Rican counterpart is composed primarily of ambivalents. This analysis will focus not on a comparison of "pure types" but on a comparison of the nature and correlates of legitimacy tensions among the sons of the establishment in the two countries. For economy in expression, however, the group tending toward support in Panama will be labeled Ambivalents since ambivalence is by far the larger component of the group, and the group tending toward opposition in Costa Rica will be labeled Ambivalents since it is composed overwhelmingly of that type with only a handful of "true" opponents. Hence the forthcoming comparisions will be among the following:

Panamanians	*Costa Ricans*
Ambivalents	Supporters
Opponents	Ambivalents

ASSESSMENT OF THE LEGITIMACY INDEX (TABLE B-1)[2]

Before embarking on an analysis of the correlates of legitimacy orientations, it is desirable to validate the index used as the base of that analysis. This will be done by examination of the relationship between the index and independent items that treat evaluations of aspects of the political system.

The only such items that focus on the political process (as opposed to the decision-makers or their policies) are two which ask whether politics and government (1) help or harm the country or neither, and (2) are honest or dishonest or neither. The variation in response according to legitimacy orientation type is in the direction expected, with the differences much stronger between the Panamanian groups than between the Costa Rican. Among the Panamanians 37 per cent of the Ambivalents held that politics helps the country and only 16 per cent said that the country is harmed; 17 per cent of the Opponents said that it helps the country while 56 per cent held that the country is harmed. Among the Costa Ricans 61 per cent of the supporters held that politics helps and only 7 per cent that it harms the country; while 46 per cent of the Ambivalents said that it helps, with 18 per cent saying that it harms. Among the Panamanians 32 per cent of the Ambivalents saw politics as "dishonest" and only 8 per cent as "honest," while 58 per cent of the Opponents said "dishonest" and 6 per cent "honest." Among the Costa Ricans there was much less negative evaluation, as 5 per cent of the Supporters stated that politics is "dishonest" and 28 per cent said "honest," while 14 per cent of the Ambivalents said "dishonest" and 18 per cent "honest."

---

[2]The following tables for this chapter are found in Appendix B, pp. 115-26.

With regard to politicians, the pattern of response was the same as the above on an item that poses an extreme proposition—"All our politicians are worthless." Among the Panamanians 47 per cent of the Ambivalents disagreed compared with 25 per cent of the Opponents. Among the Costa Ricans, a corresponding difference occurred. A less extreme proposition elicited a great deal of difference between groups. In response to the statement that "A large number of politicians sell themselves easily," 37 per cent of the Panamanian Ambivalents agreed strongly compared with 73 per cent of the Opponents; 9 per cent of the Costa Rican Supporters were in strong agreement compared with 50 per cent of the Ambivalents.

With regard to evaluation of the respective Presidents, the expected differences once again appeared. Among the Panamanians 66 per cent of the Ambivalents approved of Chiari and 18 per cent disapproved, compared with 40 per cent approval and 46 per cent disapproval by the Opponents. Among the Costa Ricans 81 per cent of the Supporters approved of Orlich and only 5 per cent disapproved, compared with 54 per cent and 28 per cent among the Ambivalents. Focus on the immediate past Presidents reveals interesting differences between the countries. In both cases, an alternation occurred between "in" and "out" parties. While 54 per cent of the Costa Rican Supporters approved the preceding President and 23 per cent disapproved, 82 per cent of the Ambivalents approved of him and only 7 per cent disapproved. Among the Panamanians, by contrast, 34 per cent of the Ambivalents approved the predecessor and 26 per cent disapproved, while 19 per cent of the Opponents approved of him and 54 per cent disapproved. Alternation of Presidents and parties certainly was related to differences in evaluation of them, but a significant aspect of this is the failure of either President to win the predominant support of the Panamanian Opponents, while legitimacy orientations in Costa Rica may well be substantially a function of partisan success, with the pattern indicating a likelihood of small shifts over time in the accordance of legitimacy. That is, both Costa Rican Presidents had predominant support among both Supporters and Ambivalents.

The evaluation of the Chiari government's effectiveness also relates to over-all legitimacy orientations. In response to the specific policy item, "The government is doing all in its power to provide adequate housing for the poor," 60 per cent of the Ambivalents and 46 per cent of the Opponents agreed. In reference to over-all performance, however, the differences were much greater. The proposition that "The government is doing a good job in solving national problems" was agreed to by 74 per cent of the Ambivalents compared with only 23 per cent of the Opponents.

Thus, responses to every item are associated with differences in legitimacy scale positions, and in the expected direction. This pattern seems to validate the scale as constructed. That is, (1) positive evaluations on individual items were associated with the higher position on the legitimacy index, and (2) the Costa Rican groups tended to make more positive evaluations than the Panamanians, which conforms to the difference in cutting points between the two groups in the two countries, between Support and Ambivalence in Costa Rica and between Ambivalence and Opposition in Panama.

EXPECTATIONS ABOUT THE NATURE OF CORRELATES OF LEGITIMACY

When we propose to analyze the covariation of legitimacy orientations with policy and ideological positions, we must have in mind some standards of difference. For example, concerning reformism we want to know if there is a consistent pattern of differences in association with differences in legitimacy orientations *and* the extent of the difference. That is, if 10 items are available to assess positions on a range of reform areas, we want to know whether a pattern of consistent differences exists with regard to all, most, half, etc. of the items. If the nature of the variation is inconsistent across the 10 items, we want to know whether at least some differences appear in the particularly crucial areas. And we want to know whether the differences are absolute, very strong, substantial, or slight. In addition, we want to know whether a consistent pattern and extent of difference occur with regard to the other theoretically relevant orientation areas, such as evaluation of alternative means to change, belief in the efficacy of alternative means to change, politicization, etc. Most of the empirical differences that social scientists have found and have used as bases for generalizations are rather small, in the sense that they explain or account for little of the variation in the major variables. In the following, we will attempt to keep these matters in mind, in order that our conclusions suffer as little as possible from either exaggeration or underemphasis.

A logically extreme case of legitimacy difference should find 100 per cent of the supporters in agreement with, for example, an ideological proposition compared with none of the opponents. However, given the multifactor determination of political orientations and behavior, we have come to look for less extreme relationships than that suggested above between any two variables. A further problem is the underdeveloped state of political theory about legitimacy; we do not know what degrees of difference empirically can lead predictably to substantial changes in the system. Consequently we can only present the actual range of differences and lack of differences, assessing them with regard to crude probabilities for stasis and change.

CORRELATES OF LEGITIMACY ORIENTATIONS

POLITICIZATION (TABLE B-2)

If the Opponents do not articulate their point of view before others or otherwise take an active part in politics, then their opposition may count for little in the calculus of political change. If despite their opposition to the system, they fail to perceive politics as involving high personal stakes, the latter conclusion would be even more strongly indicated. If the Ambivalents are little politicized in comparison with the Opposition, then the process of demoralization of the elite would seem to be more rapidly generated.

In the Panamanian case, there are no marked and consistent differences in politicization coincident with legitimacy orientations, either with respect to overt activity or psychological involvement, with one important exception. The Opponents tended to perceive the personal relevance of politics with particular intensity, as reflected in their strong disagreement with the statement, "What the government does will not affect my life very much." This suggests that the discontent underlying the Opposition will not readily be channeled into and sublimated by non-political activities, for the stakes of politics are high for these students. To the extent that the two Panamanian groups were about equally highly politicized, it is probable that whatever conflicts existed between them (and others) will be exacerbated.

In the Costa Rican case, the Ambivalents showed a somewhat higher degree of politicization on 7 of 9 indicators. This means that their political position probably weighs more than that of the

Supporters, a possible element of instability in an otherwise strongly stable picture. It remains to be seen, then, along what axes their discontent with the prevailing system is organized.

The ensuing presentation explores the nature of these discontents and conflicts.

OPPORTUNITY FOR SELF AND OTHERS (TABLES B-3 AND B-4)

Anxiety about one's future success bears no relation to support for the political system among the Costa Ricans, but there is an inverse relationship of moderate magnitude (17 to 20 per cent) among the Panamanians on 3 of the 5 items. Most of the differences tend to occur in the middle of the range, rather than at the extremes.

The Panamanian Opposition consistently (on 4 of 5 items) perceived more limitations on opportunity generally in their society than did the Ambivalents, although again most of the differences were moderate, while the Costa Ricans cannot be distinguished along this dimension, with one exception. The most substantial variation (25 and 24 per cent, respectively, in Panama and Costa Rica) occurs with reference to the perception of the openness of the political system, a matter which clearly approximates legitimacy orientation itself. With regard to the remaining aspects of the response pattern, 46 per cent of the Panamanian Opposition strongly agreed that "The good things of life are controlled by the few," but so do 32 per cent of the Ambivalents, and this is the approximate degree of the other differences along this dimension.

Thus, beliefs about opportunity for self and others form no pattern of association with legitimacy orientations of these high-status Costa Rican students. A perception of the opportunity structure as closed does seem to engender negative evaluations of the Panamanians' political system, but the nature of the differences indicates that this is but one of the factors that account for the variation in their lack of support for the system.

REFORM POSITIONS (TABLE B-5)

The Costa Rican Supporters and Ambivalents differed inconsistently from one another concerning reform, and thus this dimension does not appear to account for differences in the accordance of legitimacy to the system.

Once again, more consistent and on the whole larger differences appear between the two Panamanian groups. Almost as many Ambivalents as Opponents agreed to general principles, such as that "The rich should yield their privileges," or specific but as yet undiscussed propositions, such as "The government should provide work for all who need it." When specific controversial reform measures were posed, however, such as whether "The rich should pay much higher taxes than they do now," or especially, "This country needs a major agrarian reform," a much larger proportion of the Opposition than of the Ambivalents agreed strongly (20 and 27 per cent differences, respectively, on the latter two items). Beyond this, however, on all of these items, it should be noted that both groups were relatively evenly divided between strongly and less strongly reformist positions.

In any event, part of the Opposition among the Panamanian sons of the elite seemed to derive from anxiety over limited opportunity for self and others which promotes a political orientation of strong reformism.

NATIONALISM, THE CUBAN REVOLUTION, NEUTRALISM, AND COMMUNISM (TABLE B-6)

Ideological positions on nationalism, neutralism, and communism are at the root of legitimacy conflicts in many transitional societies. In Costa Rica, too, suspicion or antagonism toward a superordinate state, the United States, is related to legitimacy orientations, but the relationship is not consistent and is slight on the whole. The Ambivalents are somewhat less positive toward the United States—its President, programs, and private corporations—than the Supporters, but their lesser affirmation of pro-United States positions is not correlated with a leftist stance on the need for social change. Rather, this relationship may reflect some traditional elements of Latin American nationalism, such as resentment of U.S. reformism (former President Ulate of the PUN, a conservative, has opposed the socially radical planks of the Alliance for Progress as "Marxist," for example) and the U.S. cultural encroachment. At any rate, in comparison with the Panamanian case, there is in Costa Rica a muted relationship between nationalism and discontent with the political system.

A strong pattern of difference exists between the two Panamanian groups, and the strength of the difference, the absence of strong difference on some crucial items, and the nature of some of the internal group divisions along this dimension are significant. Of the 13 items that focused on aspects of national relations with the United States or the role of the United States in the region, the Opposition responded more nationalistically than the Ambivalents on every one. Four of the differences are of 30 per cent or more, 4 others are of 20 per cent or more, 2 others are of 15 per cent or more, and the remaining 3 are of 12 per cent or more.

Most Panamanians of high status appear to perceive very important common interests vis-à-vis the United States, even if they have reservations about aspects of particular policies. But a substantial proportion of the Opposition students rejected the proposition that "Essentially, Panama and the United States are good friends." Sixty per cent of the Ambivalents agreed at least substantially with the statement compared with but 23 per cent of the Opposition; 8 per cent of the Ambivalents disagreed with it compared with 42 per cent of the Opposition. Thus the Ambivalents included almost no one who denied that the two countries have an essential common interest, while the Opposition was split about evenly on the question. This suggests that the Opposition includes a substantial proportion of people who share the radical nationalist perspectives of students and intellectuals from less favored social backgrounds.

The outstanding national issue is the Canal. Only 10 per cent of the Ambivalents wanted strongly to nationalize it, in contrast with 40 per cent of the Opposition. Once again, Ambivalents included almost no radical nationalists, while the Opposition was relatively evenly divided.

A traditional nationalist issue, though of secondary importance to the Canal, has been the role of the United Fruit Company. Here, 58 per cent of the Ambivalents agreed at least substantially that "The United Fruit Company has been beneficial to the country," compared with 27 per cent of the Opposition.

A recent issue has been the hemispheric leadership of the United States in the struggle to destroy, contain, or debilitate the Cuban Revolution. The students were asked which of the following courses of action they supported with regard to the overthrow of the Castro government: action by the Organization of American States, by the United States, by the Cubans themselves, or no such action. Seventy-six per cent of the Ambivalents opted for US or OAS action; only 46 per cent of the Opposition did likewise.

Despite the consistency and strength of the difference between the Panamanian groups, there was evidence that the radical nationalist sector of the Opposition lacked confidence in itself. Though 40 per cent of the Opposition strongly supported nationalization of the Canal, only 17 per cent strongly agreed that "Panamanians can run the Canal without help from the North Americans." In this, they diverged from the sense of extreme efficacy that has characterized such dramatically successful radical nationalist movements as that led by Cárdenas in Mexico, Nasser in Egypt, Castro in Cuba, and perhaps that directed currently by the government in Rumania. On the other hand, the support given by the high-status Opposition group to the less instrumental aspects of the radical nationalist position in Panama may serve to generate self-doubt within the establishment about one of its traditional political positions and now most sensitive political commitments—essential community of interest with the United States.

The Ambivalent expressed more positive feeling than the Opponents about Presidents Eisenhower and Kennedy and the latter's Alliance for Progress. But Kennedy appears to have been evaluated by the Opponents in at least partial isolation from the Canal, United Fruit, Cuban, etc. issue areas. The large majority of the Opponents approved of him and his Alliance, and the difference in positive evaluations of Kennedy and Eisenhower was much greater among the Opponents than the Ambivalents.

These data on the range of nationalist orientations provide a context within which to evaluate the Alliance for Progress. It is clear that Kennedy was an extremely popular figure, that the Alliance was approved by both groups, and that a comparison of evaluations of Kennedy and Eisenhower indicates that Kennedy's Alliance program probably accounted for the fact that his popularity was much greater than Eisenhower's with the Opponents. In view of this, it may well be that the Alliance has made a substantial contribution toward slowing the process of disintegration of psychological ties between the United States and the Opposition youth. Without this program, which so closely fits the pattern of political preferences of the Opponents in many respects, the latter might have gone over more completely to the ranks of the country's radical nationalists.

Nonetheless, it is also clear that these positive elements have been unable to destroy the multiple bases of nationalism, at least among the Opponents. Without a local commitment and a local political mechanism, the Alliance alone could not provide resources and the spirit requisite to a telling attack on national problems. Thus, nothing was created that could serve as a national accomplishment stimulating further internal changes and developments, and reducing the tendency to make a scapegoat of the foreign enemy while ignoring local problems. Furthermore, it seems doubtful that the Alliance could have ever become a more salient program among the Panamanians than the traditionally compelling question of the Canal, unless simultaneously with the inception of the Alliance had come a renegotiation of the Canal Treaty on terms that would give Panamanians more responsibility for the operation of the enterprise. In these senses, then, the Alliance appears to have been politically and psychologically shortsighted or isolated in conception.

In preliminary presentation of this orientation dimension in Chapter IV, mention was made of the increasingly international nature of contemporary nationalism, with reference to the growing affinity for one another of the nationalist and independence movements, sometimes involving communism, in the societies striving to emerge from preindustrialism. The citizens of these societies are predominantly colored people. It was hypothesized that in the degree to which Latin American nationalism became involved with or influenced by the nationalism of "crude" and colored nations, Latin American nationalists of high status would be repelled or disinclined to participate actively in their own countries' nationalist movements.

This can be tested in part by data on orientations of the Panamanian Ambivalents and Oppositionalists toward such movements. The latter have been noted as including a substantial proportion of nationalists, while the Ambivalents have been estimated to include a much smaller proportion. If the two groups reject such types of foreign nationalism in similarly high degree, then there will be some evidence in conformity with the hypothesis.

Concerning the Cuban Revolution, which combines extremely radical nationalism with communism, both groups of students were overwhelmingly negative. Castro was evaluated negatively by virtually every one of the Opposition and by almost as high a proportion of Ambivalents. Regarding the proposition that "The Cuban Revolution is a bad example for Latin America," the ratio of agreement to disagreement is 65 to 33 among the Opposition and 60 to 40 among the Ambivalents. Furthermore, half the Opposition and only one-fourth of the Ambivalents strongly disagreed with the proposition that "It would be possible to reintegrate the Cuban government of Castro into the OAS and the inter-American family of nations." Legalization of the Communist party in Panama was strongly rejected by a very high proportion of both groups, and a large majority of both also agreed that "All Communist governments are the same." Thus neither the Cuban Revolution nor communism, local or foreign, had much appeal for these students, and on the critical issue of inter-American treatment of the Cuban government, the much more nationalist Opposition took the substantially more hostile position.

There is some evidence, too, that these high-status students were much more interested in American hemispheric affairs and even the relatively distant Cold War than in the other "have-not" peoples. They were asked to respond to equivalent statements of interest in (1) the Americas, (2) the Cold War, and (3) Africa, the Middle East, and Asia ("I am very interested in everything concerning..."). There was little difference between Ambivalents and Oppositionalists, as about half of each group expressed at least substantial interest in the Americas and in the Cold War, and only one-sixth of each the same degree of interest in Africa, etc.

Finally, the pattern of evaluations of foreign nationalists, of neutralist and communist type, and of a prominent local nationalist strongly identified with radical nationalists throughout the world provides further evidence of the limited nationalism of the Opposition students. Nasser has become widely known in Panama for his nationalization of the Suez Canal and ejection of the "imperialists" from Egypt, and Lumumba has been probably the best-known black African nationalist. Despite the hypothetically extreme importance of the Suez events for Panamanians, Nasser was strongly approved by almost no one among either the Opposition or Ambivalents. He received more total disapproval than total approval, but much more indifference than either of the above. The pattern of response to Lumumba was worth noting in detail. Sixty-three per cent of the Ambivalents and 48 per cent of the Opposition did not answer or replied "don't know," 16 per cent of the Ambivalents approved of him and 21 per cent disapproved; 4 per cent of the Opposition approved and 48 per cent disapproved. Local radical nationalist Thelma King, who is an outspoken supporter of Castro and other foreign radicals, was overwhelmingly rejected by both groups, as were, almost needless to add, Mao and Khrushchev.

The pattern clearly is one of limited nationalism among the Opposition students. Not only were they lacking in confidence about the capacity of their own nation for assertive, independent action, they also lacked interest in or were hostile to the most radical and assertive nationalist movements among the transitional societies. One may therefore predict that any affinity for such movements on the part of Panamanian nationalism will lessen its capacity to enlist the support of those sons of the establishment who are also appalled by the condition of their country.

BELIEFS ABOUT MEANS OF POLITICAL CHANGE (TABLE B-7)

Costa Rican Supporters of the system tended to diverge from Ambivalents in a few instances that suggest their greater belief in the flexibility of the system, including by inference, its capacity to accommodate utopian changes. Twenty-two per cent more of the Supporters than the Ambivalents indicated belief that "The rich can be persuaded to yield their privileges," and rejected the proposition that "Social class distinctions are inevitable." On the other hand, the two groups did not differ in response to six other items along this dimension, both groups indicating a relatively high degree of belief in the effectiveness of normal means to accommodate demands for change. Where the majority Supporters are distinguished from the others—their broader conception of possible egalitarian changes and their greater belief in the system's flexibility—perhaps suggests their contribution to the strength of the system, in that their commitments are to a system perceived to be capable of adjusting to progressive social change.

There is a set of substantial relationships (that is, a substantial relationship in a consistent direction in 6 of 9 instances) between legitimacy orientation and beliefs about means to political change among the Panamanians. Once again the exceptions to the pattern seem significant.

The Opposition tended to perceive the rich as severely constraining the officials. The thesis that "If any official really tried to resolve basic problems, the rich would prevent it" was strongly endorsed by 48 per cent of the Opponents and only 24 per cent of the Ambivalents. An equivalent difference existed concerning belief that "The rich can be persuaded to yield their privileges," and the "Legislative Assembly is very important in this country," the Opponents making the more negative assessment. More of the Opponents agreed that "Christian Democracy will be incapable of making the changes the country needs."

More of the Opponents also perceived the possibility of revolution and that it might involve personal advantages for them. While 53 per cent of the Ambivalents agreed that "A revolution like the Cuban cannot be carried out in this country," only 21 per cent of the Opponents agreed. Asked how much the Alliance, social reform, social revolution, and the maintenance of existing institutions would improve their economic situation, the two groups differed only in that 10 per cent of the Ambivalents and 33 per cent of the Opponents saw social revolution as yielding "much" improvement.

On the other hand, while the Opponents were substantially more dubious than the Ambivalents about persuading the rich to yield their privileges, just about as small a proportion of them as of the Ambivalents saw force as necessary to make them yield. This is another indication of their tendency to fail to draw the specific, painful conclusions that seem "logically" to follow from their perception of normal channels as closed to change and revolution as likely.

PREFERENCES FOR VARIOUS POLITICAL MEANS (TABLE B-8)

There is no consistent *pattern* of variation in preferences for various means by type of legitimacy orientation in the Costa Rican case. Both groups tended to support constitutional democracy and to reject effective government in favor of constitutionalism when hypothetical priorities were demanded by the questionnaire.

Given the limited bases of legitimacy conflicts encountered so far among the Costa Rican students and given the substantial differences among the three major parties of that country, it may be that legitimacy alignments follow preferences for one or another party. There are substantial differences in the partisan evaluations and alignments of the two student groups, and yet even the nature of the difference indicates the basic strength of the system insofar as these students are concerned. Evaluations of the three parties were such that the Supporters tended strongly to approve the PLN, the Ambivalents tended to approve (though not so strongly) the PUN, while neither group tended strongly to disapprove of any party. The pattern of affiliations shows that not only did the Supporters belong primarily to the PLN, but so also did the Ambivalents, so that the majority PLN recruits substantially from both groups. Party differences do seem to provide one of the few identifiable dimensions of variation in legitimacy orientations, but even these differences are far from extreme.

There is no consistent pattern of variation along this dimension with regard to the Panamanians either. There was a general shift away from constitutionalist commitments in favor of effective government from Time 1 to Time 2, and both the Opposition and the Ambivalents appear to have shifted in the same direction, though, as has been indicated in the foregoing, their political goals differ substantially. Increasing concern for effective implementation of divergent ends could of course herald increasing intra-class conflict.

There is a substantial difference between the two groups in preference for the "best solution to national problems," as 45 per cent of the Ambivalents and only 19 per cent of the Opponents opted for "capitalism." The institutionalization of some political and economic system other than the existing one would seem to require strong measures. Significantly, more Opponents than Ambivalents (52 to 34 per cent) strongly endorsed the thesis that "More than politicians, more than legislation, what this country needs is a leader in whom the people can place their confidence." There were either no differences between Ambivalents and Opponents or much greater within-group than between-group differences in regard to the appropriateness of democracy for poor countries, endorsement of freedom of speech and assembly, dissolving the existing party system, postponing elections to maintain an effective government in office, and endorsement of Christian Democracy.

On the critical question of the role of violence in political change, there were no differences between the two groups. About three-fourths rejected the use of violence to resolve political questions, and most of them believed strongly on the matter. Finally, an even larger majority endorsed the proposition that "Social change is acceptable only when it does not provoke disorder." In fact, the intensity of agreement was greater among the Opponents on this item.

Given the fact that Opponents wanted a wide variety of basic changes, it must be concluded that their preferences for political means have not been brought into line with their perception as to what means would prove effective in implementing the changes they want.

SUMMARY AND CONCLUSIONS

Those "scheduled" to inherit the establishment in Costa Rica and Panama evaluate their political systems very differently. The Costa Ricans are predominantly supportive. The minority are ambivalent, largely as a function of their negative perception of the politicians and decision-makers, rather than of the rules of the game. Almost none oppose the system. Furthermore, there are almost no orientational variations that coincide with the legitimacy dimension. That is to say, there is no delineated legitimacy conflict within this group. The one really substantial difference between Supporters and Ambivalents lies in the nature of their partisanship, and even in this respect, there is more affiliation in both groups with the majority party than any other, so that partisan divisions by no means coincide exactly with legitimacy orientations. This is even more significant in that the majority PLN is the party of the 1948 revolution, which institutionalized the basis of an egalitarian welfare state, thereby attacking the traditionally privileged. Despite this recent history, the sons of the privileged have clearly been integrated to a high degree into the political system.

The Panamanian counterparts see much less of value in their political system. Over half reject it, and very few support it. Though, as was indicated in the previous chapters, the whole group tends to perceive the need for widespread change, a perception that has markedly spread and deepened over the course of the Chiari administration, there are substantial areas of difference within the whole group about which legitimacy orientations appear to have crystallized.

There is a relationship between opposition to the system and the following: concern about one's future opportunity, perception of limited opportunity generally in the society, and reformism. The differences are by no means tremendous, however, so that one cannot conclude that these factors in themselves account for the variations in legitimacy orientation. What can be said is that more of the Opponents perceive the system as relatively closed, threatening to the level of success to which they aspire, and in need of reform. Furthermore, substantially more Opponents perceive the prevailing system as blocking changes in the desired direction and therefore perceive the probability of a major revolution occurring in the country. The Ambivalents endorse capitalism as the best solution to national problems much more than do the Opponents, whose search for change inclines them toward strong leadership as the best means to attain it. Both groups appear strongly oriented toward more effective government, but refuse at least at this point to countenance force or violence. The Opponents particularly recoil before the prospect of social disorder, despite their perception of national needs and the obstacles to their fulfillment thrown up by the existing system.

By virtue of their predisposition against coercion and risking disorder, the Opposition seems precluded from taking an active part in bringing down the existing system. But they appear to be as relatively highly politicized as the Ambivalents, more intensely aware of the stakes of politics than the latter, so that their rejection of the system, commitment to change, and belief in the probability of revolutionary change may well contribute to the downfall of that system. For this syndrome of orientations would seem probably to lead to questioning traditional assumptions and self-doubt within the elite—in short, to demoralization. Given the pattern, one might expect this large sector of privileged youth to fail to oppose strongly a movement on the part of other, less privileged citizens to make some major changes.

Inasmuch as the forces of reform, development, and "social justice" are extremely weak in Panama, however, the process of decay of the old elite would be extremely gradual, if these were the only pressures for change. But the Oppositionalist sector of the establishment youth breaks away from the system at its weakest point: its reliance on the United States. This sector is not simply or primarily reacting to the failures of the Chiari administration in the specific realms of development and social reform, but rather reacting in frustration and shame over the much more diffuse, intense matter of the defensive, weak, exploited, and corrupted condition of the nation. At a time of gathering assertiveness on the part of transitional societies all over the world, a time of profound stocktaking within Latin America largely stimulated by explosive changes in Cuba, Chiari articulated the low estate of the country generally and in detail, and then failed either to act to overcome the deficiencies or to attempt to mobilize the public support that alone might have laid the base for future action in the face of oligarchic rigidity. No outlet was provided for concern that had developed about the nation. Latin Americans of privilege have appeared to have little sense of identification or common interest with the great mass of citizens. Nationalism has tended to be the major basis for across-class unity, as the focus of attention becomes the outside enemy. The Oppositionalist sector of privileged youth in Panama reaches through nationalism its point of closest communion with students and intellectuals from other classes and with the "people" simply as fellow Panamanians, rejecting the second-class status of the country and searching for national rehabilitation.

But, just as they stop short before the prospect of coercion and risk of disorder concerning other areas of change, the Opposition also hesitates in its nationalism. They reject traditional dependency. Many strongly endorse nationalizing the Canal. But they lack confidence in their capacity to run it. Here they lose touch with emergent radical nationalism locally and internationally, which is ever more self-assertive and confident, to a degree considered "irrational" in the West. Their hesitancy is reinforced by the affinity of radical nationalism locally for the "crude and vulgar" nationalism sweeping the countries of color. But by deprecating Panama's traditional quasi-colonial status, the Opposition sector probably makes its most potent contribution to a climate of self-doubt within the establishment.

SIGNIFICANCE OF THE EMPIRICAL PATTERNS

To what degree are these findings typical of the Latin American establishment youth? The obvious answer is that there is no way to determine this at present. Beyond this, some speculation seems in order.

The Costa Rican pattern may be most unusual. The high level of support for the political system seems highly atypical for any stratum of any Latin American country. Even where classes, groups, strata have a strong interest in the status quo, the ubiquity of corruption and the manifest inadequacies of government in the face of great need engender a calculated support or acquiescence rather than positive endorsement of the system. Furthermore, the Costa Rican privileged youth value a system that has begun to institutionalize the welfare state, a process that was born in revolution. Two factors may have been critical here. The first is the ideology of the PLN, in which values have been treated as expandable and hence politics has the prospect of benefiting everyone, as opposed to being a zero-sum game.[3] This is particularly important in such cases as the Latin American, because the very longevity of their anachronistic social structures has bred fear on the part of even the slightly privileged that once begun change will be uncontrollable, a fear that a crescendo of extremist currents reinforces. The second factor is the timing of the Revolution — 1948. The significance lies in the accommodation of "the social question" and of outstanding nationalist issues before the climate of international and inter-American politics became radicalized in the 1950's. Fear of Jacobinism was probably less before Castro, before Lumumba, before

[3]Charles Anderson, "Politics and Development Policy in Central America," *Midwest Journal of Political Science,* V (November, 1961), 332-50.

Mao. Furthermore, the traditional symbol of foreign control over the economy, the United Fruit Company, was modified by the politically highly successful renegotiation of the United Fruit contract on unprecedentedly favorable terms for the Costa Ricans, thereby blunting the nationalist issue, maintaining the major industry without trauma, and producing an accomplishment affording positive national pride. This was of further importance in that anti-colonialist nationalism often focuses all political attention and energy on the external enemy, leaving undefined and unattended the problems of internal restructuring.[4] The removal of the most intense nationalist issue on a generally satisfying basis may have contributed to a more instrumental focus on internal problems in Costa Rica.

The Panamanian pattern seems more probably characteristic of the Latin American. Just how cognizant the sons of the elite are of social problems relative to other privileged youth in Latin America is extremely difficult to assess. Equally difficult to estimate are the scope of orientational changes that may have characterized counterpart groups in those few other countries where leaders of the Chiari type have arisen, men who have defined the situation as problematical but been inadequate to do anything about it. In any event, one point where the Panamanians seem most closely to parallel other groups in other countries, about whom we have only speculative assessments, is their unwillingness to sanction or even psychologically to entertain coercive action and the risk of disorder to bring about progressive changes they otherwise consider necessary and desirable. It may be that privileged youth normally shrink from coercion, violence, and disorder except where the government overtly behaves in tyrannical and bloody fashion toward them. This type of behavior on the part of Trujillo, Batista, Rojas, Somoza, etc. has provoked the taking of great risks and violent counterbehavior on the part of high-status student groups on those occasions. In the absence of such extreme socially indiscriminate provocation, youth of this social level tends to feel more stake in a very imperfect status quo than in a dimly perceived more ideal state the route to which is extremely risky and threatening. The difference in these regards between Panamanians and others may be the degree of rejection of the system and the function such rejection may perform in political change. So general and so intense are the Panamanians' beliefs in the inappropriateness of their system

[4]See the introduction to Silvert, *op. cit.*, p. 34, and the discussion of Brazilian nationalism, by Bonilla, pp. 232-64.

that they appear very likely to be generating or contributing substantially to a process of elite demoralization. A further consequence may be the disinclination or incapacity of the Opponents to resist change-oriented efforts of others, despite the fact that those others may be willing to use means far beyond those that the establishment youth would themselves sanction.

Although nationalism in the sense of hostility toward an outside enemy is extremely widespread in Latin America, its intensity and pervasiveness vary considerably. Panama represents that small set of countries where external control of the economy and general political influence have been so dominant that nationalism has been almost continuously the most salient issue, one which has grown constantly more inflammatory as the international environment has become more radicalized along this dimension. The establishment youth seem to have been much affected by this issue and promise to have a substantial effect on it themselves. As a whole, they have responded to the rise of radical nationalism locally by moving closer to the basic interest of the incumbent elite – maintaining traditional relationships with the United States. On the other hand, the Opposition has departed markedly and consistently from the traditional position, and has come to approach the local radical nationalists' position, despite the Alliance for Progress. That they are, however, doubtful of their (the country's) capacity to manage their own affairs is not surprising, since their fathers have tended to rely traditionally on the U.S. government to perform managerial functions. Despite the lack of efficacy of their nationalism, their serious questioning of this policy may weaken the resolve of the establishment on the issue on which their control of the country is most vulnerable. This relationship between nationalism in the country generally and the position of establishment youth probably occurs only where external control has been so pronounced, as, for example, was the case in Cuba. (However, a similar breadth and intensity of feeling has been triggered occasionally in less generally dominated countries when a symbolically crucial industry, such as oil, has become involved in a nationalist issue. A recent case in point is the Argentine oil concessions which were granted to North American companies by President Frondizi and which President Illia is attempting to modify. Oil exploitation has played a similar role in Brazil, Peru, and of course in Mexico during the Cárdenas presidency.)

Another factor contributing to heightened nationalism among the

Panamanian Opponents was Chiari's public development of the low estate of the country as a problem. It is conceivable that either more or less action would have been required to maintain the traditional non-nationalist orientations at least of establishment youth. That is, had Chiari mobilized the power to raise the nation from its depreciated condition, legitimacy would have soared and the resulting nationalist feeling might have been more constructive and less hostile in content, as accomplishment bolstered national pride. Or, had he simply behaved as the traditional Presidential style indicated, he would have defined no such problems, talked in no such politically charged terms, and given impetus to no such demands for national rehabilitation. In any event, the hypothesis suggests that in those countries where nationalism has played a major role, politicians tread on dangerous ground even with regard to elements of the establishment when they attempt to gain popularity by mobilizing the public on this issue without intending or being able to bring off a victory of some sort.

Even where privileged youth are drawn part-way into the nationalist camp under these conditions, however, they will probably hesitate to immerse themselves thoroughly because of the tendency of the less privileged nationalists to look outward for support from other nationalist movements in the poor, colored world. The Latin American establishment has traditionally looked to Europe for cultural leadership and has been little concerned with other areas. The new nationalism, however, promises to link low-status nations and low-status individuals within nations, particularly as a trans-national ideology of the deprived gains form and impetus. This development may be too alien for nationalists from "the better families" of Latin America.

To the extent that youth of this stratum are moved by shame over the miserable condition of the nation to reject their system, to demand changes, including changes in traditional international dependency relationships, but are unable to go all the way to support radical ideologies and radical restructuring internally and vis-à-vis formerly dominant nations, they may demoralize their incumbent elites, but find no place themselves within the ranks of those impatient to replace them.

A CONCLUDING NOTE ON THE LEGITIMACY CONCEPT

Too often in political theory it is assumed that all political systems are at least minimally legitimate. This inquiry has treated legitimacy as a major variable. At the outset, a high level of legitimacy was hypothesized to characterize only a small set of the Latin American countries, with the remainder representing a range from moderate to low levels. Costa Rica was selected for study because it seemed to present one of the rare cases of a highly legitimate system; Panama, because its system's legitimacy seemed much more problematic. Both systems have been or now are confronted by severe problems that could substantially affect their legitimacy, but despite this, some differences should appear between Panamanian and Costa Rican groups, or our concept (or operationalizing of the concept) of legitimacy would require scrapping or reformulation.

In fact, enormous variation in support for the system occurred between comparably situated groups in the two countries. Furthermore, considerable variation occurred within the Panamanian group over a relatively short period of time. The concept and its operational definition therefore seem to have useful empirical reference for comparative political theoretical research.

The utility of the concept of Ambivalence as a legitimacy orientation type seems also to have been established. Though Costa Rica and Panama vary widely in the degree of support for the system by the probable inheritors of elite positions, the distribution of support was such as to reveal a substantial middle category in both countries. This includes people who neither support nor oppose the system as a whole, but support some elements and oppose others. Our distributions were such as to preclude the isolation for analysis of another middle category of people, those who are least polarized, who acquiesce not via internal balancing of positive and negative evaluations, but by virtue of neutrality.

It seems now even more logical to hypothesize that Latin American political dynamics are largely a function of the critical variation in legitimacy orientations between Acquiescence and Opposition. But even where key elements of the population oppose the system, that system may persist, if the Opponents lack organization, self-confidence, or are immobilized at points of decision, afraid of the violence or coercion or risk that change may require. The Panamanian case suggests the hypothesis that even where the proportion of Opponents is high (for example, a majority), if the characteristics described above apply, a political system can be sustained by a very few rulers without constant overt coercion, without extreme police state methods.

APPENDIX A

TABLES FOR CHAPTERS IV AND V

THE FIRST TWO COLUMNS OF FIGURES IN THESE TABLES INCLUDE the responses of the Costa Ricans at the only time they were assessed, in 1962, and of the Panamanians at the first of two points they were assessed, in 1961 or Time 1. These two columns provide the data for Chapter IV, "Political Profiles: Time 1." The third column includes the responses of the Panamanians at the second of two points they were assessed, in 1963 or Time 2. This column, in comparison with the others, provides the data for Chapter V, "Changing Orientations: The Panamanians at Time 2."

Table A-1. EXPECTATIONS ABOUT PERSONAL SUCCESS[a]

		'62 Costa Ricans %	'61 Panamanians %	'63 Panamanians %
"I will get the job I deserve." (A-D)[b]	+3	47	46	47
	+2	36	33	37
	+1	10	10	12
	−1/−3	3	4	2
	NA/DK[c]	4	7	2
"I will never attain the success I want." (A-D)	+3/+1	4	6	6
	−1/−3	94	92	91
	NA/DK	2	2	3
"Compared to others in school, how do you see your future success?"	Among those on top	26	24	22
	Will do very well	50	53	50
	Will do all right	21	23	26
	Will not do very well	1	0	0
	NA/DK	1	0	2
"Only if things change very much will I attain the success I want." (A-D)	+3	8	8	14
	+2	7	6	13
	+1	8	11	14
	−1/−3	71	68	52
	NA/DK	6	7	6
"Only if things change very much will I attain the political influence I want." (A-D)	+3	12	13	10
	+2/+1	47	41	37
	−1/−3	38	37	44
	NA/DK	3	9	9

[a]For each item in this and the following tables in Appendix A, the responses total 100 per cent, and the *N* is always 72 for the Costa Ricans, 87 for the 1961 Panamanians, and 92 for the 1963 Panamanians.

[b]In this and the following tables, "agree-disagree" items are indicated by "(A-D)," and the responses are coded as follows: +3, strongly agree; +2, substantially agree; +1, slightly agree; −1, slightly disagree; −2, substantially disagree; −3, strongly disagree.

[c]NA/DK includes all those whose responses were not ascertained or who "don't know."

Table A-2. BELIEFS ABOUT OTHERS' CHANCES FOR SUCCESS

		'62 Costa Ricans %	'61 Panamanians %	'63 Panamanians %
"One can succeed in this country with ability and effort." (A-D)	+3	62	56	44
	+2/+1	32	40	51
	−1/−3	3	1	4
	NA/DK	3	2	0
"What is most important for success in this country?"	Hard work or skill	74	60	59
	Family position or money	25	33	40
	NA/DK	1	7	1
"The majority of the good things in life are controlled by the few." (A-D)	+3	15	30	40
	+2/+1	45	48	40
	−1/−3	39	18	19
	NA/DK	1	4	1
"There is no racial discrimination in this country." (A-D)	+3/+1	76	68	52
	−1/−3	17	29	44
	NA/DK	7	3	4
"What is most important for political success in this country?"	Hard work or pol. program	79	49	48
	Family position or money	17	47	49
	NA/DK	4	3	3

Table A-3. POLITICIZATION

		'62 Costa Ricans %	'61 Panamanians %	'63 Panamanians %
"What any government does will not affect my life very much." (A-D)	+3/+1	43	53	43
	−1/−3	51	44	55
	NA/DK	6	3	2
"How interested are you in politics?"	Very much or substantially	47	38	44
	A little	40	33	37
	Not at all	13	25	17
	NA/DK	0	3	2
"Do you intend to enter politics after you leave school?"	Yes	22	23	30
	No	72	74	68
	NA/DK	6	3	2
"How often do you talk about politics or government with:				
Family	Frequently	26	42	40
	Occasionally	46	28	36
	Never	25	28	21
	NA/DK	3	2	3
School friends	Frequently	39	36	28
	Occasionally	48	47	41
	Never	10	15	28
	NA/DK	3	2	3
Friends outside the school	Frequently	19	23	20
	Occasionally	51	52	49
	Never	26	23	28
	NA/DK	3	2	3
"How often do you talk about the Cuban Revolution?"	Frequently	49	62	37
	Occasionally	49	36	57
	Never	1	1	7
	NA/DK	1	1	0
"Did you attend any meetings in relation to the recent election campaign?"	Yes	50	29	31
	No	50	68	68
	NA/DK	0	3	1
"Have you taken an active part in any student demonstrations within the past few years?"	No	18	31	39
	Yes, in some	64	55	46
	Yes, in many	17	13	14
	NA/DK	1	1	1

Table A-4. Evaluation of the Political System

		'62 Costa Ricans %	'61 Panamanians %	'63 Panamanians %
"Government and politics:"	Helps the country	54	54	27
	Hurts the country	11	19	37
	Neither	33	25	35
	NA/DK	1	2	1
"Government and politics are:"	Honest	24	22	8
	Dishonest	8	22	44
	Neither	67	54	46
	NA/DK	1	2	2
"With what political party are you affiliated?" (Costa Ricans' party affiliations and evaluations below)	None	21	47	56
	A party mentioned	79	53	44
"The majority of the public officials work in behalf of the public welfare." (A-D)	+3/+1	61	32	17
	−1/−2	26	38	39
	−3	11	26	42
	NA/DK	1	3	2
"A great many politicians sell themselves easily." (A-D)	+3	25	51	57
	+2	14	26	24
	+1	22	13	12
	−1/−3	36	9	6
	NA/DK	3	1	1
Evaluation of the President	Strong approval	26	38	10
	Approval	44	49	43
	Disapproval/strong disap.	14	4	32
	NA/DK	15	9	15
Evaluation of the preceding President	Approval/strong approval	65	47	26
	Disapproval/strong disap.	17	31	42
	NA/DK	18	22	32
"The government is doing a good job in resolving basic problems." (A-D)	+3	–[a]	22	10
	+2	–	29	11
	+1	–	32	26
	−1/−3	–	14	41
	NA/DK	–	3	12

(continued on next page)

Table A-4. EVALUATION OF THE POLITICAL SYSTEM (continued)

		'62 Costa Ricans %	'61 Panamanians %	'63 Panamanians %
"The government is doing all it can to provide adequate housing for the poor." (A-D)	+3	–	45	13
	+2	–	28	14
	+1	–	16	26
	−1/−3	–	9	43
	NA/DK	–	2	3
"All our politicians are worthless." (A-D)	+3	10	–	27
	+2	8	–	11
	+1	14	–	24
	−1/−3	68	–	37
	NA/DK	0	–	1
"In general our system of government and politics is good for the country." (A-D)	+3	36	–	4
	+2	36	–	18
	+1	19	–	18
	−1/−3	7	–	58
	NA/DK	1	–	2

Party affiliation (Costa Ricans only) (percentaged across)	PRN	PUN	PLN	Other	None
Respondent's party	14	21	43	1	21
Respondent's father's party	17	31	40	1	11
Respondent's best friends' party	10	8	65	0	17
Evaluation of the parties (Costa Ricans only)					
Strongly approve	8	17	37		
Approve	20	26	24		
Indifferent	22	32	17		
Disapprove	26	6	7		
Strongly disapprove	13	1	8		
NA/DK	11	18	7		

[a]In this and the following tables, where an item was not included in the particular part of the study reported on, the omission is marked by (–).

Table A-5. Reform Positions

		'62 Costa Ricans %	'61 Panamanians %	'63 Panamanians %
"The government should provide work for all who need it." (A-D)	+3	53	63	64
	+2/+1	36	30	24
	−1/−3	8	6	12
	NA/DK	3	1	0
"This country needs a great agrarian reform." (A-D)	+3	25	41	53
	+2/+1	49	46	37
	−1/−3	21	9	9
	NA/DK	6	3	1
"The rich should pay much higher taxes than they pay now." (A-D)	+3	19	25	38
	+2	13	12	17
	+1	28	17	14
	−1/−3	36	40	31
	NA/DK	4	6	0
"Do you believe the rich should give up their privileges?"	Yes	36	–	61
	No	58	–	36
	NA/DK	6	–	3

Table A-6. NATIONALISM, THE CUBAN REVOLUTION, AND COMMUNISM

		'62 Costa Ricans %	'61 Panamanians %	'63 Panamanians %
"Essentially this country and the United States are good friends." (A-D)	+3	51	23	13
	+2	42	39	27
	+1	3	26	31
	−1/−3	1	8	28
	NA/DK	3	4	1
"Do you like, dislike, or feel indifferent toward North Americans?"	Like	67	33	29
	Dislike	6	15	22
	Indifferent	24	50	43
	NA/DK	4	2	6
Evaluation of President Kennedy	Strongly approve	81	51	43
	Approve	15	44	32
	Disapprove/strongly dis.	1	1	14
	NA/DK	3	4	10
"North American corporations should not be permitted to operate in this country." (A-D)	+3/+1	37	36	32
	−1/−2	33	38	39
	−3	28	26	28
	NA/DK	1	0	1
"The United Fruit Company is beneficial for this country." (A-D)	+3/+1	79	71	79
	−1/−3	18	24	17
	NA/DK	3	5	4
"If the job were good, I would like to work for a North American company in this country." (A-D)	+3/+2	74	45	50
	+1	11	24	16
	−1/−3	15	26	32
	NA/DK	0	5	2
"The Panama Canal should be nationalized." (A-D)	+3	14	29	28
	+2/+1	39	24	17
	−1/−3	43	44	54
	NA/DK	4	3	1
"The Panamanians can run the Canal without any help from the United States." (A-D)	+3/+1	–	34	28
	−1/−3	–	60	72
	NA/DK	–	6	0
"In 10 years the strongest country in the world will be:"	USA	72	45	52
	USSR	11	31	13
	China/Neutrals	13	16	29
	NA/DK	4	8	6

(continued on next page)

Table A-6. NATIONALISM, THE CUBAN REVOLUTION, AND COMMUNISM (continued)

		'62 Costa Ricans %	'61 Panamanians %	'63 Panamanians %
"The Cuban Revolution is a bad example for Latin America." (A-D)	+3	58	58	42
	+2/+1	15	20	20
	−1/−3	21	20	36
	NA/DK	6	3	2
Evaluation of Fidel Castro	Approval/strong approval	1	5	3
	Disapproval	11	10	19
	Strong disapproval	83	80	70
	NA/DK	4	5	8
"The Communist Party should be declared legal." (A-D)	+3/+1	10	1	9
	−1/−2	8	2	7
	−3	81	96	84
	NA/DK	1	1	0
"Concerning action to overthrow Fidel Castro, I would accept action by:"	No one or only Cubans	26	48	34
	USA or OAS	71	52	59
	NA/DK	3	0	7

Table A-7. BELIEFS ABOUT MEANS OF POLITICAL CHANGE

		'62 Costa Ricans %	'61 Panamanians %	'63 Panamanians %
"Social class distinctions are inevitable." (A-D)	+3/+1	60	63	79
	−1/−2	18	21	12
	−3	12	14	9
	NA/DK	10	2	0
"There is not much difference between our political parties." (A-D)	+3/+1	37	59	71
	−1/−3	57	34	27
	NA/DK	6	7	2
"If any public official tried to resolve basic problems, the rich would prevent it." (A-D)	+3	11	29	37
	+2	18	19	18
	+1	21	13	19
	−1/−3	46	37	24
	NA/DK	4	2	2
"A revolution like the Cuban could not be carried out in this country." (A-D)	+3/+1	69	62	35
	−1/−2	14	21	32
	−3	13	16	26
	NA/DK	4	1	7
"Christian Democracy will be incapable of making the changes the country needs." (A-D)	+3/+1	–	6	13
	−1/−2	–	34	47
	−3	–	58	37
	NA/DK	–	2	3
"Do you believe the rich can be persuaded to yield their privileges?"	Yes	56	–	54
	No	39	–	41
	NA/DK	5	–	4
"Do you believe force will be necessary to make the rich yield their privileges?"	Yes	21	–	34
	No	74	–	62
	NA/DK	5	–	3
"The Legislative Assembly is very important in this country." (A-D)	+3	61	–	33
	+2/+1	36	–	55
	−1/−3	1	–	11
	NA/DK	1	–	1
"How much is it possible to improve your economic situation by means of the following:" (each alternative presented independently)	% replying "much"			
	Alliance for Progress	68	–	31
	Social reform	33	–	43
	Social revolution	4	–	22
	Maintenance of existing institutions	26	–	21

Table A-8. EVALUATION OF MEANS OF POLITICAL CHANGE

		'62 Costa Ricans %	'61 Panamanians %	'63 Panamanians %
"Democracy is inappropriate for poor countries." (A-D)	+3/+1	15	14	24
	−1/−2	20	18	24
	−3	61	68	49
	NA/DK	4	0	2
"Freedom of speech and assembly should be unlimited." (A-D)	+3/+1	61	38	45
	−1/−3	39	62	53
	NA/DK	0	0	2
"Violence should never be used to resolve political questions." (A-D)	+3	56	51	53
	+2/+1	24	23	22
	−1/−3	19	25	25
	NA/DK	1	1	0
"The political parties should be dissolved." (A-D)	+3/+1	11	23	33
	−1	8	15	19
	−2	21	20	17
	−3	53	40	27
	NA/DK	7	2	4
"If a government is doing a good job, it should be allowed to continue in office, even if it means postponing elections." (A-D)	+3/+1	29	43	54
	−1	6	10	6
	−2	8	9	6
	−3	57	36	31
	NA/DK	0	2	3
"Christian Democracy represents the formula for resolving national problems." (A-D)	+3	–	59	37
	+2/+1	–	34	46
	−1/−3	–	6	12
	NA/DK	–	1	5
"More than legislation, more than politicians, what this country needs is a leader in whom the people can place their confidence." (A-D)	+3	25	–	46
	+2	14	–	19
	+1	7	–	9
	−1/−3	51	–	23
	NA/DK	3	–	3
Best solution for national problems:	Capitalism/Indig. soc.	75	–	40
	Marxism/others	7	–	29
	NA/DK	18	–	31
"Social change is acceptable only when it does not provoke disorder." (A-D)	+3/+1	68	–	71
	−1/−3	19	–	18
	NA/DK	13	–	11

APPENDIX B

TABLES FOR CHAPTER VI

Table B-1. ASSESSMENT OF THE LEGITIMACY INDEX[a]

		C.R. Sup. %	C.R. Ambiv. %	Pan. Ambiv. %	Pan. Opp. %
"Government and politics:"	Helps country	61	46	37	17
	Hurts country	7	18	16	56
	Neither	30	36	45	27
	NA/DK	2	0	2	0
"Government and politics are:"	Honest	28	18	8	6
	Dishonest	5	14	32	58
	Neither	65	68	55	36
	NA/DK	2	0	5	0
"All our politicians are worthless." (A-D)	+3/+1	28	39	53	73
	−1	14	21	16	6
	−2/−3	58	39	31	19
	NA/DK	0	0	0	2
"A great many politicians sell themselves easily." (A-D)	+3	9	50	37	73
	+2/−3	88	50	61	27
	NA/DK	2	0	3	0
Evaluation of the President	Approval/strong app.	81	54	66	40
	Disap./strong disap.	5	28	18	46
	NA/DK	14	18	16	14
Evaluation of the preceding President	Approval/strong app.	54	82	34	19
	Disap./strong disap.	23	7	26	54
	NA/DK	23	11	40	27
"The government is doing all it can to provide adequate housing for the poor." (A-D)	+3/+1	–		60	46
	−1/−3	–		37	50
	NA/DK	–		3	4
"The government is doing a good job in resolving basic problems." (A-D)	+3/+1	–		74	23
	−1/−3	–		21	60
	NA/DK	–		5	17

[a]For each item in this and the following tables in Appendix B, the responses total 100 per cent, and the *N* is always 43 for the Costa Rican Supporters, 28 for the Costa Rican Ambivalents, 38 for the Panamanian Ambivalents, and 48 for the Panamanian Opponents.

Table B-2. POLITICIZATION

		C.R. Sup. %	C.R. Ambiv. %	Pan. Ambiv. %	Pan. Opp. %
"What any government does will not affect my life very much." (A-D)	+3/+1	42	46	50	38
	−1/−2	32	29	34	23
	−3	21	21	16	35
	NA/DK	5	4	0	4
"How interested are you in politics?"	Very much/substantially	44	54	47	44
	A little	44	32	32	42
	Not at all	12	14	18	14
	NA/DK	0	0	3	0
"Do you intend to enter politics after you leave school?"	Yes	19	29	34	27
	No	74	71	66	69
	NA/DK	7	0	0	4
"How often do you talk about politics or government with:"					
Family	Frequently	23	29	42	42
	Occasionally	44	50	39	33
	Never	28	21	16	21
	NA/DK	5	0	3	4
School friends	Frequently	35	46	21	33
	Occasionally	51	43	47	38
	Never	9	11	29	25
	NA/DK	5	0	3	4
Friends outside the school	Frequently	14	29	13	23
	Occasionally	51	50	53	48
	Never	30	21	32	25
	NA/DK	5	0	3	4
"How often do you talk about the Cuban Revolution?"	Frequently	44	54	37	36
	Occasionally	54	43	55	60
	Never	2	0	8	4
	NA/DK	0	4	0	0
"Did you attend any meetings in relation to the recent election campaign?"	Yes	58	36	34	27
	No	42	64	66	71
	NA/DK	0	0	0	2
"Have you taken an active part in any student demonstrations within the past few years?"	No	21	14	32	44
	Yes, in some	65	64	53	39
	Yes, in many	14	22	13	17
	NA/DK	0	0	3	0

Table B-3. Beliefs about Personal Success

		C.R. Sup. %	C.R. Ambiv. %	Pan. Ambiv. %	Pan. Opp. %
"I will get the job I deserve." (A-D)	+3	44	54	40	50
	+2	47	21	42	33
	+1	5	18	18	8
	−1/−3	2	4	0	4
	NA/DK	2	4	0	4
"I will never attain the success I want." (A-D)	+3/+1	7	0	5	6
	−1/−2	44	50	39	36
	−3	49	50	53	54
	NA/DK	0	0	3	4
"Compared to others in school, how do you see your future success?"	Among those on top	28	21	32	17
	Will do very well	47	57	50	48
	Do all right/not very well	23	21	16	33
	NA/DK	2	0	2	2
"Only if things change very much will I attain the success I want." (A-D)	+3/+1	25	21	40	48
	−1/−3	70	71	60	42
	NA/DK	5	7	0	10
"Only if things change very much will I attain the political influence I want." (A-D)	+3/+1	65	54	42	50
	−1/−3	33	43	55	35
	NA/DK	2	4	3	15

Table B-4. BELIEFS ABOUT OTHERS' CHANCES FOR SUCCESS

		C.R. Sup. %	C.R. Ambiv. %	Pan. Ambiv. %	Pan. Opp. %
"What is most important for success in this country?"	Hard work or skill	74	71	66	52
	Family position or money	26	25	32	48
	NA/DK	0	4	2	0
"What is most important for political success in this country?"	Hard work or pol. program	88	64	63	38
	Family position or money	10	29	37	58
	NA/DK	2	7	0	4
"There is no racial discrimination in this country." (A-D)	+3/+2	70	75	39	25
	+1/−3	21	21	53	73
	NA/DK	9	4	8	2
"The majority of the good things in life are controlled by the few." (A-D)	+3	16	14	32	46
	+2/−3	81	86	68	52
	NA/DK	2	0	0	2
"One can succeed in this country with ability and effort." (A-D)	+3	63	64	45	44
	+2	33	18	45	37
	+1/−3	5	14	10	19
	NA/DK	0	4	0	0

Table B-5. Reform Positions

		C.R. Sup. %	C.R. Ambiv. %	Pan. Ambiv. %	Pan. Opp. %
"Do you believe the rich should give up their privileges?"	Yes	42	29	58	67
	No	53	64	39	29
	NA/DK	5	7	3	4
"The government should provide work for all who need it." (A-D)	+3	60	43	60	65
	+2/−3	40	54	40	35
	NA/DK	0	4	0	0
"The rich should pay much higher taxes than they now pay." (A-D)	+3	16	25	26	46
	+2/−3	81	71	74	54
	NA/DK	2	4	0	0
"This country needs a great agrarian reform." (A-D)	+3	23	29	40	67
	+2/−3	72	64	60	31
	NA/DK	5	7	0	2

Table B-6. NATIONALISM, THE CUBAN REVOLUTION, NEUTRALISM, AND COMMUNISM

		C.R. Sup. %	C.R. Ambiv. %	Pan. Ambiv. %	Pan. Opp. %
"Essentially this	+3/+2	98	86	60	23
country and the	+1	2	4	32	33
United States are	−1/−3	0	4	8	42
good friends." (A-D)	NA/DK	0	7	0	2
"The Panama Canal	+3		–	10	40
should be	+2/−3		–	90	58
nationalized." (A-D)	NA/DK		–	0	2
"The United Fruit	+3/+2	51	43	58	27
Company is bene-	+1/−3	44	57	42	67
ficial for this country."	NA/DK	5	0	0	6
(A-D)					
"Concerning action to	No one or only Cubans	30	21	21	44
overthrow Fidel	USA or OAS	70	71	76	46
Castro, I would accept	NA/DK	0	7	3	10
action by:"					
"The Panamanians	+3		–	3	17
can run the Canal	+2/+1		–	13	17
without any help from	−1/−3		–	84	67
the United States."	NA/DK		–	0	0
(A-D)					
Evaluation of	Strongly approve	18	36	18	10
President Eisenhower	Approve	63	39	45	25
	Disapprove/str. disap.	12	18	16	44
	NA/DK	7	7	21	21
Evaluation of	Strongly approve	88	68	53	35
Kennedy	Approve	7	29	29	33
	Disapprove/str. disap.	0	4	8	21
	NA/DK	5	0	11	11
"Have you changed	Yes, relations better	79	68	74	54
your opinion about	No, relations still good	21	21	10	13
Pan./C.R.-U.S.	Yes, relations worse	0	4	5	10
problems because of	No, relations still bad	0	0	8	23
the Alliance for	NA/DK	0	7	3	0
Progress?"					

(continued on next page)

Table B-6. NATIONALISM, THE CUBAN REVOLUTION, NEUTRALISM, AND COMMUNISM (continued)

		C.R. Sup. %	C.R. Ambiv. %	Pan. Ambiv. %	Pan. Opp. %
"Nationalization of the Canal would mean a better life for most Panamanians." (A-D)	+3/+2		–	21	42
	+1/–3		–	76	54
	NA/DK		–	3	4
"Only nationalization of the Canal will bring real independence to Panama." (A-D)	+3		–	13	35
	+2/–3		–	87	65
	NA/DK		–	0	0
"If the job were good, I would like to work for a North American company in this country." (A-D)	+3/–2	93	89	92	79
	–3	7	11	5	19
	NA/DK	0	0	3	2
"North American corporations should not be permitted to operate in this country." (A-D)	+3/–2	65	79	63	75
	–3	33	21	37	23
	NA/DK	2	0	0	2
"Do you like, dislike, or feel indifferent toward North Americans?"	Like	67	64	37	25
	Dislike	2	11	18	25
	Indifferent	26	21	42	44
	NA/DK	5	4	3	6
Evaluation of Fidel Castro	Approve/strongly app.	0	4	3	4
	Disapprove/str. disap.	95	93	84	92
	NA/DK	5	4	13	4
"The Cuban Revolution is a bad example for Latin America." (A-D)	+3/+1	72	75	60	65
	–1/–3	23	18	40	33
	NA/DK	5	7	0	2
"It would be possible to reintegrate the Castro government into the OAS and the inter-American family of nations" (A-D)	+3/–2		–	74	40
	–3		–	26	48
	NA/DK		–	0	12

(continued on next page)

Table B-6. NATIONALISM, THE CUBAN REVOLUTION, NEUTRALISM, AND COMMUNISM (continued)

		C.R. Sup. %	C.R. Ambiv. %	Pan. Ambiv. %	Pan. Opp. %
"The Communist Party should be declared legal." (A-D)	+3/−2	19	18	8	21
	−3	79	82	92	79
	NA/DK	2	0	0	0
"All Communist governments are the same." (A-D)	+3/+1	84	75	68	71
	−1/−3	12	21	32	27
	NA/DK	5	4	0	2
"I am very interested in everything concerning the other American countries." (A-D)	+3/+2	68	71	58	50
	+1/−3	30	29	39	50
	NA/DK	2	0	3	0
"I am very interested in everything concerning the Cold War." (A-D)	+3/+2	49	36	50	50
	+1/−3	44	57	47	44
	NA/DK	7	7	3	6
"I am very interested in everything concerning Africa, the Middle East, and Asia." (A-D)	+3/+2	28	43	16	17
	+1/−3	65	57	84	79
	NA/DK	7	0	0	4
Evaluation of Nasser	Approve/strongly app.	9	18	13	23
	Disapprove/str. disap.	33	43	32	29
	NA/DK	58	39	55	48
Evaluation of Lumumba	Approve/strongly app.		–	16	4
	Disapprove/str. disap.		–	21	48
	NA/DK		–	63	48
Evaluation of Thelma King	Approve/strongly app.		–	8	8
	Disapprove/str. disap.		–	79	83
	NA/DK		–	13	8
Evaluation of Mao	Approve/strongly app.		–	0	6
	Disapprove/str. disap.		–	79	67
	NA/DK		–	21	27
Evaluation of Khruschchev	Approve/strongly app.	2	4	3	10
	Disapprove/str. disap.	89	96	89	81
	NA/DK	9	0	8	9

Table B-7. BELIEFS ABOUT MEANS OF POLITICAL CHANGE

		C.R. Sup. %	C.R. Ambiv. %	Pan. Ambiv. %	Pan. Opp. %
"If any public official tried to resolve basic problems, the rich would prevent it." (A-D)	+3	11	11	24	48
	+2/−3	84	86	76	48
	NA/DK	5	3	0	4
"Do you believe the rich can be persuaded to yield their privileges?"	Yes	65	43	68	46
	No	30	50	32	46
	NA/DK	5	7	0	8
"The Legislative Assembly is very important in this country." (A-D)	+3	65	57	45	27
	+2	21	39	45	40
	+1/−3	12	4	10	31
	NA/DK	2	0	0	2
"Christian Democracy will be incapable of making the changes the country needs." (A-D)	+3/−1		—	26	42
	−2/−3		—	71	54
	NA/DK		—	3	4
"A revolution like the Cuban could not be carried out in this country." (A-D)	+3/+1	72	64	53	21
	−1/−3	21	36	47	69
	NA/DK	7	0	0	10
"How much is it possible to improve your economic situation by means of the following:" (each alternative presented independently)	% replying "much"				
	Alliance for Progress	65	71	37	29
	Social reform	30	39	45	44
	Social revolution	0	11	10	33
	Maint. of exist. insts.	28	21	21	23
"Do you believe force will be necessary to make the rich yield their privileges?"	Yes	21	18	29	36
	No	77	71	71	58
	NA/DK	2	11	0	6
"There is not much difference between our political parties." (A-D)	+3/+1	39	32	79	65
	−1/−3	56	61	21	31
	NA/DK	5	7	0	4
"Social class distinctions are inevitable." (A-D)	+3/+1	53	71	82	77
	−1/−3	40	18	18	23
	NA/DK	7	11	0	0

Table B-8. PREFERENCES FOR VARIOUS POLITICAL MEANS

Party evaluation (Costa Ricans only)	PRN Sup. %	PRN Amb. %	PLN Sup. %	PLN Amb. %	PUN Sup. %	PUN Amb. %
Strong Approval	5	14	49	21	14	21
Approval	19	18	28	18	23	32
Indifferent	21	25	14	18	35	25
Disapproval	33	18	5	11	7	4
Strong Disapproval	12	14	0	21	2	0
NA/DK	12	11	5	11	19	18

Party affiliation (Costa Ricans only)	PRN	PLN	PUN	Other	None
Supporters %	7	49	21	0	23
Ambivalents %	21	36	21	4	18

		C.R. Sup. %	C.R. Ambiv. %	Pan. Ambiv. %	Pan. Opp. %
Best solution for national problems:	Capitalism	47	57	45	19
	Marx., Indig. socialism, Marxism + capitalism	37	36	10	29
	Other + other combin.	7	4	21	17
	NA/DK	9	4	24	35
"More than legislation, more than politicians, what this country needs is a leader in whom the people can place their confidence." (A-D)	+3	23	29	34	52
	+2/−3	72	71	63	46
	NA/DK	5	0	3	2
"Democracy is inappropriate for poor countries." (A-D)	+3/+2	12	4	16	15
	+1/−1	7	21	8	19
	−2/−3	79	68	76	62
	NA/DK	2	7	0	4
"Freedom of speech and assembly should be unlimited." (A-D)	+3	37	18	13	23
	+2/−2	35	68	55	33
	−3	28	14	29	42
	NA/DK	0	0	3	2

(continued on next page)

Table B-8. PREFERENCES FOR VARIOUS POLITICAL MEANS (continued)

		C.R. Sup. %	C.R. Ambiv. %	Pan. Ambiv. %	Pan. Opp. %
"The political parties should be dissolved." (A-D)	+3	7	4	3	17
	+2/−2	32	39	76	42
	−3	56	50	21	33
	NA/DK	5	7	0	8
"If a government is doing a good job, it should be allowed to continue in office even if it means postponing elections." (A-D)	+3/+1	23	36	55	52
	−1/−2	12	18	13	11
	−3	65	46	29	33
	NA/DK	0	0	3	4
"Christian Democracy represents the formula for resolving national problems." (A-D)	+3		–	32	42
	+2/−2		–	63	52
	−3		–	0	10
	NA/DK		–	5	6
"Violence should never be used to resolve political questions." (A-D)	+3	58	54	53	52
	+2/+1	26	18	26	19
	−1/−3	16	25	21	29
	NA/DK	0	4	0	0
"Social change is acceptable only when it does not provoke disorder." (A-D)	+3	14	14	18	33
	+2/+1	58	50	61	35
	−1/−3	19	22	18	17
	NA/DK	9	14	3	15

APPENDIX C

THE ASSESSMENT OF RESPONSE SET

RESPONSE SET IS THE TENDENCY OF SOME PEOPLE TO ASSENT TO propositions made to them in a questionnaire or interview context, and of others to reject propositions, regardless of the content of the propositions. The problem was not really satisfactorily accommodated in this research design, however, in that the questionnaire contained few sets of items the substance of which was the same but the form of which was reversed, thereby serving as a check on the internal validity. If one hypothesizes that response set occurs generally for some people and only occasionally for others, then a relatively large number of such sets of items are required as tests. Only two sets composed of two items each and widely dispersed throughout the questionnaire were concluded to be satisfactory as tests of response set. One pair was common to both the Panamanian and Costa Rican questionnaires. The other pair varied in substance.

The pair common to both asked for evaluation of politicians; the other pair asked in Costa Rica for an evaluation of the President and in Panama for an evaluation of the Christian Democratic movement. All four items had the same general format: a statement with which the respondent was asked to agree, strongly, somewhat, or slightly, or disagree, strongly, somewhat, or slightly. The items were as follows:

The majority of the public officials work in behalf of the people's welfare.
A great number of politicians sell themselves easily.

Costa Rica only:

Don Francisco Orlich will carry out a job of great value for the country.
I do not expect Orlich to be a good president.

Panama only:

Christian Democracy represents the formula for resolving national problems.
Christian Democracy will be incapable of making the changes the country needs.

These pairs consist of items so nearly opposed in meaning and so unambiguous as to serve present purposes well.

Originally another pair of items in the same format and dealing with an aspect of nationalism had been selected in addition to tap response set. It is described here as an illustration of the difficulty of constructing post hoc controls for the problem. The items, in both Costa Rican and Panamanian questionnaires, were:

North American companies should not be permitted to operate in this country.
If the job were good, I would like to work for a North American company here in [Panama, Costa Rica].

Focusing on ideology, it appears at first that the items contradict one another: one cannot oppose local operations of U.S. companies and also accept employment from them, and vice versa. But this is an imposed "rationality," for the nationalist syndrome may well involve a rejection of foreign corporations in the abstract but an avidity for the income and fringe benefits provided by their employment. Or, variation on the theme, it may involve a long-term perspective, combining hostility toward the United States with an inclination to take everything one can get from U. S. sources before the "inevitable" seizure or ouster of these enterprises. (There is, to my knowledge, no even remotely systematic information available on the orientations toward nationalism of local employees of U. S. firms in Latin America, which would seem an important matter suggested by the considerations above.) Similarly, a Latin American student (particularly conceivable of the upper-class respondent) may logically reject the first statement, thereby affirming the desirability of U. S. firms' operating in the country, while also rejecting the second statement because one personally does not want the types of employment made available therein. In any event, the degree of obviously logical contradiction between these nationalist items from the standpoint of the student respondent seems much less than that for the two previous pairs, and for this reason they were judged unsatisfactory as indicators of response set.

The decision was made to hold separate in the analysis those who failed to demonstrate content sensitivity to the two selected sets of items. However, content sensitivity is not an absolute; it ranges empirically from an extreme of sensitivity to an extreme of response set. The range was measured as follows. On each item, there were six categories of response, ranging from strong agreement through strong disagreement, as previously described. This range was scored:

Not ascertained–	0
Strong agreement–	1
Some agreement–	2
Slight agreement–	3
Slight disagreement–	4
Some disagreement–	5
Strong disagreement–	6

The two subscales were based on the following scores per pair of items:

High assenter	1 or 2 on one item and 1 or 2 on the other
Low assenter	3 on one item and 1, 2, or 3 on the other
Content sensitive	1, 2, or 3 on one item and 4, 5, or 6 on the other
Low rejector	4 on one item and 4, 5, or 6 on the other
High rejector	5 or 6 on one item and 5 or 6 on the other
Not ascertained	0 on either item

The respondents were located on the general scale of response type according to the combination of responses on the two subscales, as indicated in Table C-1.

Table C-1. GENERAL SCALE OF RESPONSE TYPE: SUMMARY FREQUENCY DISTRIBUTION

Scores and Scale Type	C.R. '62 No.	C.R. '62 %	Pan. '61 No.	Pan. '61 %	Pan. '63 No.	Pan. '63 %
0 on both subscales: Not Ascertained	2	1.7	6	4.1	0	0.0
Content sensitive on both subscales; Content sensitive on one, 0 on other Content sensitive on one, low assenter on other; Content sensitive on one, Low rejector on other: Content Sensitive	72	59.5	87	60.0	90	78.9
All other combinations: Response Set	47	38.8	52	35.9	24	21.1
Total	121	100.0	145	100.0	114	100.0

Tables C-2, C-3, and C-4 show that the major response set problem is assent. There are very few respondents who fail to answer the relevant items and almost none who consistently reject regardless of content. This pattern provides further evidence of the generally cooperative response of the students to the project, inasmuch as failure to respond or "indiscriminate" rejection would seem the more likely channels through which to express hostility. In response to the new, politically focused questionnaire situation, the general tendency was to cooperate, but where the content was too difficult to comprehend or to permit of decision, or lacking in salience, the easiest answer, agreement, was given. Interestingly enough, comparable data from students of middle- and working-class background fall into the same pattern with regard to direction of response set—assent rather than non-response or rejection. Thus, if it is a correct hypothesis that this is a reflection of cooperativeness toward the study, it suggests not only the broad possibilities for collection of data from intellectual groups that are widely considered to be hostile both to North Americans and to scientifically oriented social research, but also that large initial samples must be acquired because the incidence of response set within the generally cooperative environment of data collection tends to be high.[1]

[1]A general analysis of response set among students of varying class background has been made; see my "Response Set in Political Survey Research on Costa Rican and Panamanian Students: A Comparative Analysis" (dittoed).

Table C-2. General Scale of Response Type: Total Frequency Distributions, Costa Rica 1962

		"POLITICIANS" SUBSCALE							
		NA	CS	HA	LA	LR	HR	Total	%
	NA	2	3	1	2			8	6.6
	CS	2	36	11	22	5	4	80	66.1
"ORLICH"	HA		4	3	2			9	7.4
SUBSCALE	LA		2	2	9	1	1	15	12.4
	LR		2	2	3			7	5.8
	HR	1		1				2	1.7
Total		5	47	20	38	6	5	121	100.0
%		4.1	38.8	16.5	31.4	5.0	4.1		99.9

Key: NA – Not Ascertained
CS – Content Sensitive
HA – High Assenter
LA – Low Assenter
LR – Low Rejector
HR – High Rejector

Table C-3. General Scale of Response Type: Total Frequency Distributions, Panama 1961

		"POLITICIANS" SUBSCALE							
		NA	CS	HA	LA	LR	HR	Total	%
	NA	6	2		2			10	6.9
	CS	3	55	19	23	2	3	105	72.4
"CHRISTIAN	HA	2	6	2	7	1		18	12.4
DEMOCRACY"	LA	1	1	4	1			7	4.8
SUBSCALE	LR		1					1	.7
	HR		3	1				4	2.8
Total		12	68	26	33	3	3	145	100.0
%		8.3	46.9	17.9	22.8	2.1	2.1		100.1

Key: NA – Not Ascertained
CS – Content Sensitive
HA – High Assenter
LA – Low Assenter
LR – Low Rejector
HR – High Rejector

Table C-4. GENERAL SCALE OF RESPONSE TYPE: TOTAL FREQUENCY DISTRIBUTIONS, PANAMA 1963

		"POLITICIANS" SUBSCALE							
		NA	CS	HA	LA	LR	HR	Total	%
	NA		6	1				7	6.1
	CS	3	54	4	14	3	1	79	69.3
"CHRISTIAN	HA	1	4					5	4.4
DEMOCRACY"	LA	1	5	2	3			11	9.6
SUBSCALE	LR		5			2		7	6.1
	HR		5					5	4.4
Total		5	79	7	17	5	1	114	99.9
%		4.4	69.3	6.1	14.9	4.4	.9		100.0

Key: NA – Not Ascertained
CS – Content Sensitive
HA – High Assenter
LA – Low Assenter
LR – Low Rejector
HR – High Rejector

Thus, weighing the need to eliminate response set to reduce the chances of making spurious statements and the need to maintain a sample size sufficient for the projected analysis, the cutting point was established between those (1) who demonstrated content sensitivity on one subscale and something less than a high degree of response set on the other, and (2) all others.

It is clear from the frequency distributions that the assenting response set varies by country, by the substance of the items (salience), and over time (in Panama). Though there are many whose response set is limited to an area of low salience, there are many others who seem generally to assent. In addition, a comparison of the content sensitive and the assenting based on the general scale shows a widespread tendency (especially pronounced among the Costa Ricans) of the latter to select the first response category throughout the questionnaire, again with the item content varying widely in such a manner that the first response category cannot be regarded as a substantively consistent reaction to the questionnaire stimulus. But given the limitations of this study and the failure to include in the research design instruments for the collection of data on correlates of general and partial response set, no more can be said here of factors associated with the various types.

Some additional comments seem in order regarding variations in response set. There is considerable variation between the subscales, in that the score on one is a relatively poor predictor of the score on the other. Thus, the salience of the substantive area of inquiry seems established as a source of variation. Extreme content sensitivity ("appropriately" combined agree and disagree responses on both pairs of items) ranges from some 30 per cent among the Costa Ricans to some 47 per cent among the Panamanians questioned in 1963. On the other hand, there is almost no incidence of extreme set (a high assenting or high rejecting combination of responses on both pairs). This means that many respondents cluster around the midpoints of the continuum, rendering difficult the decision as to the location of cutting points for the typology of responses.

The comparatively low salience or intensity of politics in Costa Rica may be indicated by the relatively high incidence of assent on the "Politicians" subscale. However, the data on political participation reflect somewhat more involvement of the Costa Rican student than the Panamanians (in 1961), so that assent on this subscale cannot by itself be taken as an indicator of the comparative politicization of the samples.

The increasing salience of "politicians" seems to account in large part for the decreasing assent over time in the samples from Panama. The rather sharp increase in the Panamanians' content sensitivity is also associated with heightened politicization in some of its aspects. Interestingly enough, the rise in politicization occurs with regard to measures of orientations rather than overt behavior, which in fact declines, indicating that the perceived political environment of these Panamanian students may be becoming more constraining as their evaluations of the political system become more negative.

INDEX

INDEX

INDEX

PRINTED IN U.S.A.